LOOK AGAIN

LOOK AGAIN

Recognize Your Worth

Renew Your Hope

Run with Confidence

TIM TEBOW

WITH **A.J. GREGORY**

NELSON BOOKS
An Imprint of Thomas Nelson

Look Again

Copyright © 2025 by Timothy R. Tebow

All rights reserved. No portion of this book may be reproduced, stored in a retrieval system, or transmitted in any form or by any means—electronic, mechanical, photocopy, recording, scanning, or other—except for brief quotations in critical reviews or articles, without the prior written permission of the publisher.

Published by Nelson Books, an imprint of Thomas Nelson, 501 Nelson Place, Nashville, TN 37214, USA. Nelson Books and Thomas Nelson are registered trademarks of HarperCollins Christian Publishing, Inc.

Thomas Nelson titles may be purchased in bulk for educational, business, fundraising, or sales promotional use. For information, please email SpecialMarkets@ThomasNelson.com.

Unless otherwise noted, Scripture quotations are taken from The Holy Bible, New International Version®, NIV®. Copyright © 1973, 1978, 1984, 2011 by Biblica, Inc.® Used by permission of Zondervan. All rights reserved worldwide. www.Zondervan.com. The "NIV" and "New International Version" are trademarks registered in the United States Patent and Trademark Office by Biblica, Inc.®

Scripture quotations marked CSB® are taken from the Christian Standard Bible®, Copyright © 2017 by Holman Bible Publishers. Used by permission. Christian Standard Bible® and CSB®, are federally registered trademarks of Holman Bible Publishers.

Scripture quotations marked *The Message* are taken from THE MESSAGE. Copyright © 1993, 2002, 2018 by Eugene H. Peterson. Used by permission of NavPress. All rights reserved. Represented by Tyndale House Publishers, Inc.

Scripture quotations marked NASB are taken from the New American Standard Bible® (NASB). Copyright © 1960, 1962, 1963, 1968, 1971, 1972, 1973, 1975, 1977, 1995 by The Lockman Foundation. Used by permission. www.lockman.org

Scripture quotations marked NET are taken from Scripture quoted by permission. Quotations designated (NET©) are from the NET Bible® copyright ©1996–2017 by Biblical Studies Press, L.L.C. http://netbible.com All rights reserved.

Emphasis in Scripture quotations has been added by the author.

Certain names have been changed to protect individuals' privacy.

Any internet addresses, phone numbers, or company or product information printed in this book are offered as a resource and are not intended in any way to be or to imply an endorsement by Thomas Nelson, nor does Thomas Nelson vouch for the existence, content, or services of these sites, phone numbers, companies, or products beyond the life of this book.

ISBN 978-1-4002-5420-0 (HC)
ISBN 978-1-4002-5462-0 (audiobook)
ISBN 978-1-4041-2182-9 (custom)
ISBN 978-1-4002-5743-0 (custom signature edition)
ISBN 978-1-4002-5461-3 (ePub)

Without limiting the exclusive rights of any author, contributor or the publisher of this publication, any unauthorized use of this publication to train generative artificial intelligence (AI) technologies is expressly prohibited. HarperCollins also exercise their rights under Article 4(3) of the Digital Single Market Directive 2019/790 and expressly reserve this publication from the text and data mining exception.

HarperCollins Publishers, Macken House, 39/40 Mayor Street Upper, Dublin 1, D01 C9W8, Ireland (https://www.harpercollins.com)

Library of Congress Cataloging-in-Publication Data

Names: Tebow, Tim, 1987- author | Gregory, A. J., 1976- author
Title: Look again : recognize your worth. Renew your hope. Run with confidence. / Tim Tebow with A. J. Gregory.
Description: Nashville, Tennessee : Thomas Nelson, [2025] | Summary: "New York Times bestselling author Tim Tebow shares a dynamic message on identity, meaning, and purpose"-- Provided by publisher.
Identifiers: LCCN 2025025793 | ISBN 9781400254200 hardcover | ISBN 9781400254613 ebook
Subjects: LCSH: Christian life
Classification: LCC BV4501.3 .T425 2025 | DDC 248.4--dc23/eng/20250811
LC record available at https://lccn.loc.gov/2025025793Art direction: Darren Samuel

Art Direction: Darren Samuel
Cover Design: Micah Kandros
Interior Design: Kristy Edwards

Printed in the United States of America
25 26 27 28 29 LBC 5 4 3 2 1

To our daughter, Daphne Reign. May you always know your God-given worth, live with the hope of eternity, and run with confidence because you know whose you are and who you're running to.

CONTENTS

A Note from Tim..viii
Introduction... xi

PART 1: RECOGNIZE YOUR WORTH

Chapter 1: Life Unworthy of Life...................................... 5
Chapter 2: Image Is Everything...................................... 21
Chapter 3: The Truth of Who We Are 31
Chapter 4: Our Royal Reality....................................... 41
Chapter 5: When Royalty Goes Wrong 57
Chapter 6: The Royal Rescue 67
Chapter 7: What Our Royal Status Means...................... 81

PART 2: RENEW YOUR HOPE

Chapter 8: Jesus in the Margins.................................... 101
Chapter 9: God's Image—No Exceptions......................... 119
Chapter 10: Royalty in Rubble 133

PART 3: RUN WITH CONFIDENCE

Chapter 11: A Royal Response 153
Chapter 12: Lives on the Line.. 167
Chapter 13: Another Look 185

Acknowledgments 199
Notes 201
About the Authors..217

A NOTE FROM TIM

IF YOU'VE PICKED UP THIS BOOK, I WANT TO START by saying something really simple—but really important: Thank you.

Thank you for being willing to open something that I know at times won't always be easy to read. This book will take you on a roller coaster of emotions. You'll be challenged and inspired. You'll also read some hard things—stories that aren't easy to take in. But I also want you to find hope—in the highs, the lows, the moments of darkness and light, and in the journey that connects them all.

Some of what's in this book is heavy. It's painful. It's not the kind of content you can skim over casually. These are real stories. Real people. Real suffering. And that weight? It matters.

Even the process of putting this book together came with tension. There were a lot of discerning conversations about how deep we chose to go, knowing that I didn't write this to make people comfortable. I wrote it to bring light. To bring perspective. And, ultimately, to bring hope.

Because avoiding pain doesn't heal it. Ignoring injustice doesn't stop it. But naming it and facing it with faith and courage is what uncovers hope. And that changes everything.

There will be moments when this book challenges you. But I want you to know that on every page, in every story, there is hope. The book of Hebrews reminds us we have a hope that is an anchor for our soul—firm and secure. That anchor doesn't disappear in the darkness. It holds us steady. If the gospel ended at the cross, this would be a book without hope. But thank God, it doesn't end there. The grave couldn't contain the reason we have hope. And that's why this book doesn't end in despair either.

Even when you can't see it—hope.

Even when you don't feel it—hope.

Even when the pain is loud—hope.

My prayer is that you will find hope in who you are, how God sees you, and how you can see others. If you want to see yourself and see others differently . . .

If you're facing heartbreak . . .

If you want to believe that your life—and the lives of others—really matter, no matter what the world says . . .

You've picked up the right book.

INTRODUCTION

THE HAUNTING SOUND RIPPED THROUGH THE Haitian village, silencing the birds. The women walking froze midstride, ears locked on the noise. Could it be an injured dog? Maybe a goat? As the wailing rose, the women quickened their pace, weaving through thickets and darting between brush. Then, at the sound's peak, they froze, the color draining from their faces.

The cry didn't belong to an animal; it came from a baby boy.

Frantzky lay on a thin mattress on a worn porch, his clubbed feet twisted inward. The stained fabric sagged through splintered wooden planks, fistfuls of worn-out stuffing bursting through broken seams. Frantzky's skeletal body writhed as mosquitos bit at his skin. Neighbors told the women his mother had likely gone to the market, so the women waited for her on the porch. They took turns cradling the severely malnourished baby. His mom didn't return until the next day.

The women would soon learn that this "baby" was actually three years old. Weighing only thirteen pounds, Frantzky was the size of a four-month-old infant. Ravaged by sickness, this boy had clubbed feet, a drug-resistant strain of malaria, and significant neurological problems that led to serious developmental issues. He would never walk or talk on his own. Overwhelmed by his special needs, Frantzky's mother had tried to abandon him several times. As in many other cultures across the world, in her community children with special needs face deep stigma, often viewed as supernaturally cursed. Fearing shame, families often hide these children or abandon them on doorsteps or in trash cans.

The women who found Frantzky were part of a Haitian ministry we've partnered with, led by incredible friends. Though these people took measures to educate and support his mom, she had no desire to care for him, so he came under the care of myLIFEspeaks, an organization that works closely with Haitian Child Services to create infrastructure so abandoned and neglected children don't fall through the cracks. During the next six years, Frantzky received intensive physical and nutritional therapy and medical intervention to treat his malaria as well as surgery to correct his clubbed feet. Whenever I'd visit, I'd carry Frantzky around with me, rarely putting him down. He'd thrust his arms around my neck and hold on as tight as he could, which wasn't very much considering his limited dexterity. Despite his medical needs, joy seeped from his spirit. Even today I can still feel the warmth from Frantzky's smile. Stretching from dimple to dimple, it was his trademark. He wore it all the time. Softening hearts, spreading warmth, he impacted countless lives with his smile alone.

When Frantzky was about nine years old, he fell gravely ill. Unable to keep any food down and after forty-eight hours of vomiting, he was rushed to a local clinic. The moment the medical staff took one look at Frantzky's disabled body, they turned him away. He was raced to a nearby hospital, where once again he was turned away at the door. A second hospital admitted him reluctantly, but within hours it was clear the staff wasn't giving Frantzky the care he desperately needed. By the time he was transferred to a third hospital, it was too late. Left ignored and untreated for so long, his symptoms worsened. He died within minutes of arriving.

I don't know what was worse—Frantzky dying from a likely treatable virus or being treated like a virus, seen as if he was the problem.

The way people looked at Frantzky is both shocking and heartbreaking. Or should I say, the way they *wouldn't* look at him. For most of us, reading about the plight of a helpless and abandoned child stirs something deep within us. It's an emotional wake-up call. But let's zoom out for a bit.

I want to ask you a question that's challenged me over the past fifteen years, one I can't shake: How do you see people? I'm not talking about just surface stuff but how you view them at your core. Do you measure their worth by social status or achievements? By what they can give or do for you? Do you define people by their flaws or failures? Does their value stem from their talent or connections?

What if I told you there was a way to look at people that would change everything? I mean *everything*, and that's not hyperbole.

> I want to ask you a question that's challenged me over the past fifteen years, one I can't shake: How do you see people?

Launched in April 1990 at the cost of $1.6 billion, the Hubble Space Telescope was designed to show the world just how stunning space is. As of February 2024, the most famous telescope in the world has made more than one million observations revealing super massive black holes, new stars being born, and galactic collisions. You can find Hubble's discoveries in every modern astronomy textbook.[1]

Few remember that Hubble was nearly a total flop.

The images from the 1990 launch came back blurry. The promise of jaw-dropping, spectacular pictures? Far from it. What should have been crystal-clear views of the galaxies were hazy and unimpressive images. The most famous telescope in the world became the punch line not only in the space community but in the general population. From Congress to late-night television, NASA's embarrassing blunder fueled countless jokes.

Hubble's problem was a flaw in its primary mirror, the heart of the telescope. It couldn't focus.[2] For the brightest stars astronomers could tweak the images with software, but when it came to the dimmer corners of the universe, Hubble needed a fix, or, more simply put, new glasses.[3] The problem and its solution were monumental. Just how much was at stake? One astrophysicist said, "If the Hubble repair is a failure, we can write off space science for the foreseeable future."[4]

In 1993, NASA launched a servicing mission to manually repair the telescope. It was the last chance to turn the entire space program around. In just eleven days, and with a record-breaking five spacewalks, the telescope's focus was corrected.

With the fix in place, Hubble looked again into the vastness of space, unveiling galaxies, stars, and a beauty that had always been there yet had been unseen in its full glory. The difference between those new images and the ones from just three years earlier was mindblowing. As remarked in NASA's January 1994 press conference after the repair, "The trouble with Hubble is over."[5] You might call it the greatest comeback in scientific history.

You can have the best equipment in the world, but if the basics aren't in place, none of it matters. Just as this telescope's tiny flaw distorted its ability to see the cosmos clearly, our view of people becomes distorted when we judge them based on hollow, unreliable, and faulty standards instead of seeing them through God's eyes.

When God looks at you, me, and everyone else, He sees beyond physical appearance. Beyond cultural norms and labels. Beyond what someone has or doesn't have, beyond what someone can or cannot do, beyond physical and neurological restrictions and limits that are self-imposed. It's why Jesus could look at the marginalized, the forgotten, and the overlooked and find beauty, value, and worth every time.

One of the most life-changing aspects of my faith has been how God opened my eyes to see the true value of people—especially those the world overlooks, marginalizes, or judges. This shift in perspective, spurred on by a bumper sticker you'll read about in a later chapter, has deeply shaped my journey. It has become the heart behind everything I do. And in this book, I am going to share that heart with you.

Look Again is the result of three years of intense study and research, but more than that, it's a testament to how God has challenged and impacted me through vulnerable people. This book is also an invitation to join me in coming to grips with one of the most important human truths, a truth I've only recently been able to articulate. I can finally reveal what I believe God has shown me in my heart and what the world must know.

When I look back at some of my biggest regrets, those moments I wish I could take back, I realize that so often I didn't see people the way God sees them. I missed their worth. I didn't carry the hope I should have shared. And that's my prayer for you: that you would be open to learning from my mistakes. I hope that my daughter, Daphne, and all the children Demi and I may have will one day look back at the things I pursued and what I devoted my time, my heart, and my energy to and be proud of their daddy. I want them to be proud not of the things I did but of how I saw people like Jesus does.

Because here's the truth: When your eyes are cloudy, your heart gets cloudy too. When you don't see people with the worth God's given them, it's easy to react out of pride, anger, or fear. But when you see them through His eyes, it makes all the difference. You carry hope. You treat others with the love and value they deserve. When we see ourselves and others clearly, we begin to recognize the worth He's placed in you and in everyone around you. And when you do, it will change how you live, how you love, and how you make a difference in this world.

This book is divided into three parts:

Recognize Your Worth: Understanding what it means to be created in the image of God and an ancient truth of how God sees us.
Renew Your Hope: Uncovering the undeniable reality of who others are and the hope that's promised even through difficulties, challenges, and trauma.
Run with Confidence: Recognizing our urgent responsibility to protect, defend, and fight for the worth of others.

Transformation starts by recognizing your worth. And I'm not talking about the kind of worth the world hands out based on status, success, or how many likes you get. I'm talking about the real thing. The kind of worth that comes from the One who made you. And when that truth sinks into your soul, it ignites something powerful: hope. A real, unshakable hope that isn't dependent on your circumstances but anchored in who God says you are. It's the hope that reminds you that God has done something incredible for you. He's redeemed you, called you by name, and given you a purpose. That kind of hope changes everything. When you recognize your worth and embrace the

> When you know how deeply you're loved, you can step forward boldly, even when the odds are stacked against you.

hope that comes from God's truth, you can't help but run with confidence. Not because everything in your life is perfect but because you know the One who holds your future. And when you know how deeply you're loved, you can step forward boldly, even when the odds are stacked against you.

I've seen this happen with some of the trafficking survivors I've met, women who have been through unimaginable pain and darkness but are now flourishing again with confidence. They've caught hold of that hope, and it's transformed their lives. They're pursuing their dreams, taking steps forward, and making a difference.

I'm inviting you on that kind of journey. Because when you truly grasp the worth God placed on you from the beginning, you can cling to lasting hope through hard times and bring that hope to a hurting world.

In this book I tackle some bone-deep, heartbreaking topics and evils, including trafficking, exploitation, and laws that have wrecked lives. I also share stories of people who have taught me so much about how God loves and sees each one of us.

But hold on: This book isn't just about other people. It's also about the one reading this book—you. The only way to begin to see and treat others the way God does is to understand and embrace how He sees us. And man, how many times have I fallen short!

> The only way to begin to see and treat others the way God does is to understand and embrace how He sees us.

NASA astronaut Story Musgrave, payload commander of Hubble's repair mission, once said this about space: "You look to the heavens for what the meaning of life is down here. . . . It tends to shed a light on who we are. And who humanity is."[6]

Musgrave recognized Hubble as a bridge between the heavens and our understanding of ourselves, but the real connection isn't just in the stars. The truth is, the Creator of the universe designed the blueprint for who we are—and I can't wait to walk alongside you as we unlock this life changer in the pages to come.

By the time you reach the end of this book, I hope you'll be able to look again and answer this question with confidence: How do you see people? My prayer is that your answer will be: "Like God does."

Frantzky was born into a world of hatred and indifference. His funeral, however, painted a very different picture. The entire village filled the streets to honor his precious life. Even his mother came. And in what can only be described as a God-ordained moment of reconciliation and a sign of deep love and respect, she offered to bury in their family tomb the son she had abandoned.

Frantzky was finally seen the way God had always seen him.

Sometimes I wonder what might have happened if the doctors who dismissed him had chosen to look again, beyond his disability. What if so much of the world's suffering comes from not seeing ourselves and others the way God sees us? So, let me ask you: What would change if you truly saw yourself through God's eyes? How would it transform your self-image, your choices, your hope, and your confidence? And what if you could see others the same way? How would that impact how you love, serve, and bring healing to a hurting world?

As we dive in, I want to start where history and humanity collide—with a story of some of the lives of those the world has cast aside. This first chapter belongs to the history books, a history I hope will never be repeated.

Part 1

RECOGNIZE YOUR WORTH

YOUR WORTH DOESN'T COME FROM WHAT YOU DO, FROM WHAT YOU'VE DONE, OR WHAT'S BEEN DONE TO YOU. IT COMES FROM WHO MADE YOU.

Chapter 1

LIFE UNWORTHY OF LIFE

THERE ARE ONLY TWO ROOMS IN THE HOUSE where my wife, Demi, and I live where I have any say in how things look. The first is the gym, which is in our garage. The other is the TV room, where we watch movies and, of course, catch college football games. Both rooms are easy places to lose perspective, the TV room most of all. I'll walk in, put on a game, and before I know it—especially if the University of Florida is playing and losing—I'm sucked into the story unfolding on the screen. I can get so worked up that I lose my cool, and that low-key anger lingers all day. That's not an exaggeration. No matter how many times it's happened (and trust me, it's a lot), it still feels nearly impossible not to get supercharged over stuff that in the grand scheme holds little to no value. I knew things had to change to help level out my perspective.

AN MVP LENS

Right by the door of the TV room, I hung a beautiful portrait of Frantzky, the boy you met in the introduction. Our friends at myLIFEspeaks knew how much I loved this little boy and gave the painting to me as a gift after he passed away. Every time I walk into or out of that room, I see Frantzky. His hallmark smile, pushed high by his dimpled cheeks, takes center stage. A silver crown studded with colorful jewels rests above his eyebrows, hinting at a worth far greater than what society thought of him. When you see his face, you're immediately drawn in.

Seeing this picture helps remind me of what truly matters. Some days I miss the mark, but I keep trying—both in life and in that TV room—to focus on what's bigger than a game, a score, a win, or a loss.

In 2011, I wrote my first book, *Through My Eyes*. Looking back, my eyes had not been fully opened to what I needed to see. Yes, that book certainly shared a look into my life then, but over the last thirteen years I have learned valuable lessons, many at the expense of my own failures, disappointments, and insecurities about my image. While I may have chased after the title of MVP (the sports acronym for "most valuable player") along with championships, awards, and accolades many years ago, God has since opened my eyes to pursue the more important MVP—the *most vulnerable people*. These MVPs are the children, men, and women who have been viewed as less than, insignificant, or cursed and have been thrown away, abandoned, trafficked, exploited, or orphaned.

When I was fifteen and on a mission trip, I met Sherwin, a boy in the jungles of the Philippines whose feet were turned backward. Because of his disability, this little boy was seen as what I mentioned above: a throwaway, insignificant, and cursed by the people in his community. That day I knew Sherwin wasn't a throwaway to God, and by extension he shouldn't be to me. Meeting that boy was the first time God ignited in me a passion and vision to fight for the real MVPs. I want to spend the rest of my life fighting for the most vulnerable people. It's one of my greatest honors.

A NEW TIME

In 2023, the Olympic Stadium in Germany was used to host the 2023 Special Olympics, welcoming 7,000 athletes with intellectual disabilities from more than 170 nations to compete in 26 summer sports. I not only had the opportunity to attend but I also helped host and share the stories of some of these incredible athletes. To say it was emotional would be an understatement.

One of my favorite moments was getting to walk with these men and women from all over the world during the Parade of Athletes in the Opening Ceremony. Some athletes beamed with wide grins, others held back tears, and all of them soaked up the moment when for once the world's eyes were on them celebrating their achievements. When I looked at the faces of the athletes with special needs, their families, and their coaches, I saw pure and unfiltered joy radiating throughout that stadium. I remember thinking it was a picture of worship. It wasn't a church service, but the beauty of God's creation was being glorified. Being able to attend and help host the Special Olympics in Berlin felt like truth, renewed hope, and redemption rolled into a few days.

The highlight of being in Berlin for the Games was meeting some truly remarkable athletes. Like seventy-year-old Loretta Claiborne, chief inspiration officer of the Special Olympics. This was her ninth time competing since she first joined in 1970, at just the second Special Olympics ever held. When I met her, she was competing in tennis. Loretta also has a deep passion for knitting and patiently tried to teach me a thing or two. Unfortunately, I more or less created a jumble of tangled yarn. (You're a great teacher, Loretta—sorry I wasn't the best student!)

Loretta passionately spoke about her desire to change the attitudes of people toward those with special needs. She said, "If we're given a chance . . . we can do anything we want to give back to the community. We want to be a part of society. We want to get an education. And the only way we could do that is for society to look at us as people." Echoing millions of men, women, and children around the world, she reminded us, "My disabilities do not define who I am."[1]

My buddy Charlie Phillips, a powerlifter from Missouri, is another inspiring athlete. He was born with incorrectly positioned organs and hypotonia, a condition causing low muscle tone. Having spent years in and out of hospitals, he was once told by doctors that he would never walk. Charlie proved them wrong.[2] When he was eleven, he participated in his first Special Olympics USA Games in track and field, representing the state of Pennsylvania. Charlie came home from the 2023 World Games with four medals for powerlifting. He said, "I definitely beat the odds . . . my dream has come true."[3]

Another special moment was watching track and field superstar Marcelino Lages from Brazil being fitted with a special hearing aid. For the first time in his life, he could hear, and in this instance, he heard a crowd cheering for him.[4] Wow! I can't even begin to imagine what that must have been like for Marcelino.

I was also incredibly blessed and psyched to meet a student named Alejandra at Tebow Down, one of our ministries in Guatemala that serves children with developmental disabilities. I wasn't as excited, though, when she gave me a thumbs-down after I showed her my gymnastic moves. Oh well, there's a reason she's the Olympic gymnast and I've been cut from football teams a bunch of times.

Innocentia Msikinya, a table tennis competitor from one of my favorite countries, South Africa (I'm biased, of course, since my wife is South African), also inspired me. She enjoyed crushing me when we played a quick one-on-one game. As a professional nail technician, Innocentia loves getting to talk to people and ask all about them while she does their nails. She told me she's so grateful to the Special Olympics for including athletes of all abilities.

What an honor for me to get to share stories with the world and watch history unfold.

I'm inspired by the motto of the athletes in the Special Olympics Germany: "Nothing about us without us having a say,"[5] a slight twist on a common saying in the disability community. In other words, nothing was going to happen to them without their say-so. The statement was a personal declaration of worth and a claim of ownership over their lives. God would agree. He might even put His own spin on it: "Nothing about anyone without My say about them."

Just a few miles or a short car ride away from the Olympic Stadium stands a quiet memorial that I'll never forget. It's a 24-meter-long wall of blue-tinted glass, stretching beside a bus terminal. At first glance, it might not look like much. But it tells the story of something unimaginable. This wall honors the memory of hundreds of thousands of men, women, and children with disabilities who were murdered under the Nazi regime's "T4 euthanasia program." While Adolf Hitler's atrocities against the Jewish people are widely known, fewer know who he targeted first: people with special needs. Before ordering the extermination of the Jewish population, Hitler sought to eliminate children and adults he deemed unworthy of life to begin creating what was in his mind the master race, an Aryan nation he called the "highest image of God."[6] What a horrible perversion of the biblical phrase meant to highlight the inherent worth of every human being.

In 1936, the Olympic Games took place in Germany. And while the world cheered for incredible athletes, behind the scenes darkness was spreading. The Nazi government was already sterilizing people they didn't consider "fit" to belong to their vision of a superior race. Jewish citizens were being stripped of rights, segregated, and silenced.

And the foundations of a much greater evil were being quietly laid. When the Games were over and the rest of the world retreated to their corners, the same stadium was used multiple times for speeches and rallies to promote Nazi ideology.

What you're about to read isn't easy. It wasn't easy to write either. But don't look away. Stay with me. Because just like the gospel didn't end at the cross, your story—our story—doesn't end in the dark. The grave didn't get the final word, and neither does pain. We're headed somewhere . . . so let's walk through this together.

> Just like the gospel didn't end at the cross, your story—our story—doesn't end in the dark.

THE COST OF BEING UNFIT

In 1920, a German psychiatrist named Alfred Hoche and attorney Karl Binding wrote a book titled *Allowing the Destruction of Life Unworthy of Life*. The work is just as sick as the title suggests. The authors argued that certain individuals—particularly those with severe disabilities or chronic illnesses—have no worth or right to live. Championing eugenic ideology, a set of beliefs and practices to improve the genetic quality of a human population through selective breeding or elimination, Hoche and Binding advocated the practice of "mercy deaths."[7]

Viewed as a launching pad for Nazi genocide policies, this eugenic work normalized dehumanizing people with disabilities, promoting the extinction of "useless eaters," as cruelly deemed by the authors.[8] Hoche and Binding proposed that people with intellectual disabilities, or who they identified as "mentally dead," were no more than excess baggage to be dumped.[9] They believed that killing people with disabilities wasn't truly taking a life, as they saw them as lacking intelligence and emotional capacity, no more than simple animals.

Hoche and Binding downplayed concerns raised by this twisted mindset. They assured readers that mercy killings for people with disabilities were acts of "higher civil morality" that stemmed "from the deepest compassion."[10] Simply put, killing this population was the kind and the right thing to do. *Allowing the Destruction of Life Unworthy of Life* was a hit, quickly releasing two editions within two years.[11] It's no surprise that Hitler and fellow Nazi leaders embraced the eugenic ideology and made it their own in the form of racial hygiene.[12]

It's important to note that Hoche and Binding were not members of the Nazi Party. Nor were they socialists. Experts in their disciplines, they belonged to the academic world. These authors envisioned a future starkly different from their modern era, which valued preserving all life, no matter how "worthless." In this imagined "new time,"[13] a new morality would emerge, where an individual's worth was measured by their contribution. The deliberate elimination of people with disabilities who required "heavy sacrifices" would become not only accepted but necessary.[14]

Thirteen years later this new time had come.

A FUTURE DENIED

In January 1933, less than six months after Hitler came to power, he enacted the eugenic-inspired Law for the Prevention of Offspring with Hereditary Diseases. This legislation, drawn up by a committee consisting of respected medical doctors, geneticists, public health officials, and legal experts, mandated involuntary sterilization of people with the following physical and mental disabilities: hereditary feeblemindedness, blindness and deafness, schizophrenia, manic-depressive disorder, Huntington's, and severe physical deformity.[15] At least 375,000 Germans were sterilized under this law and as many as 20,000 people died from complications relating to the procedure.[16]

Forced sterilization wasn't a legislative mandate confined to the borders of Germany. Starting in 1907, about 60,000 people were sterilized in the United States, most of whom were individuals living in institutions, deemed "mentally ill" or "mentally deficient."[17] Reproductive experts at the time viewed sterilization as a way of lessening or eliminating the social and financial burden of caring for "degenerate stock."[18] The state of Indiana passed the world's first law mandating sterilization. More states followed. By 1932, a total of thirty-two states had passed laws permitting the government to sterilize the "insane," "feebleminded," "dependent," and "diseased."[19] One advocate praised these so-called surgical solutions, referring to them as "a science devoted to the improvement of the human race through better breeding."[20] To date, eight states have issued official apologies.[21]

This is important history. It's also largely forgotten history. But in every way, when we stop seeing people as fully human, horrible things ensue. For Hitler, exterminating the potential for life that was deemed unworthy before it could even begin wasn't enough. Eugenics played a part in another of Hitler's laws for racial hygiene. In 1935, he enacted the Marital Hygiene Law, which forbade "healthy" Germans from marrying anyone with "diseased, inferior, or dangerous genetic material."[22] According to his autobiography, *Mein Kampf,* marriage should produce only able-bodied and mentally fit offspring, or what he termed "images of the Lord and not monstrosities halfway between man and ape."[23]

Do you hear how evil twists the truth about God's image into something horrible?

T4: OFFICIAL EUTHANASIA BEGINS

In mid-1939, the Nazi government secretly began planning the systematic killing of children with disabilities. This program, known as "T4," was initiated by Hitler just two years before the broader genocide of European Jews in what he called the "Final Solution."[24] The term *euthanasia*, which traditionally means "good death," was distorted by the Nazis to mask a mission of murder.[25] Eventually the T4 program expanded to include teenagers and adults.

On August 18, 1939, the "Requirement to Report Deformed etc. Newborns" was issued, ordering physicians, midwives, and nurses to report all infants born with specified medical conditions: Down syndrome, blindness, deafness, microcephaly, hydrocephalus, physical deformities like missing limbs and spine or skull defects, and paralysis.[26]

The wording of this law was purposely misleading. It suggested that the objective for this reporting was to collect information and help answer scientific questions rather than its true goal of obtaining names of people who were to be murdered. The form proved insufficient, and in June 1940 another form was released requiring additional information, including the child's religion, address, and medical histories.

Upon receipt the forms were sent to three medical experts, who were tasked with deciding the fate of these children. Assessments were made without examining the children or accessing their medical records. A plus sign (+) on a form indicated death, a minus (-) for life or postponement of death. The children with the plus sign were sent to state hospitals under the guise of "being cured," instead of the evil truth that they were marked for death.[27] Parents who questioned the process faced threats of losing their custodial rights.[28]

LOOK AGAIN

Some children with disabilities were poisoned; others were starved. Many doctors in these hospitals chose to let these kids die from so-called natural causes, often by withholding care to ensure a slow and painful death. It also made for a more realistic death certificate. One physician was known for giving tours of his hospital to expose the "biological deficiency" of his pediatric patients with disabilities. One individual on such a tour testified that this doctor once plucked a child out of its crib and held it up in his hand like a dead rabbit. Praising the benefits of death by starvation as "much simpler and far more natural," the doctor held the "whimpering skeleton" and said something like, "With this one, for example, it will still take two to three days."[29] At least twenty-two killing wards like this one were eventually discovered.[30] I'd like to tell you about a few of these children.

One child named Robert suffered from a shattered hip due to a complicated birth. The injury wasn't noticeable until he turned four. In an interview years later, he shared how when his mom brought him to the doctors, she overheard a disturbing conversation in which one doctor said he "would do away with" Robert by giving him a needle and putting the child to sleep. Alarmed that a physician would kill her child, Robert's mother fled the office with her son. She and Robert led a life on the run for years.[31]

Seven-year-old Erwin wasn't so lucky. Born with Down syndrome, he died in a killing center in April 1943. His fake cause of death was listed as pneumonia. Also listed on the record were the words *Jew* and *mongolism*, a term used to describe someone with Down syndrome.[32]

Max developed meningitis early in childhood and became deaf and intellectually delayed. He was killed when he was fourteen. A note in his file said he was "unlikely ever to be able to work."[33]

Starting with children, Hitler and the Nazi regime set in motion a broader plan to purge Germany of what it labeled "life unworthy of life."[34] On September 21, 1939, just a month after the initial decree to kill children with disabilities, the murder of adults with disabilities was officially initiated.[35]

Adult victims of the euthanasia program included patients in nursing homes, mental hospitals, and long-term care facilities. In 1939, mental hospitals housed more than three hundred thousand patients. In 1940, the number dropped to forty thousand.[36] A professor working in one of the psych wards grew concerned about the future of the medical field. "With all the mentally ill being eliminated, who will want to pursue studies in the burgeoning field of psychiatry?"[37]

Patients who survived the kill list managed to pass a standard of mental and physical capacity set alarmingly high to prove value via function. For example, even if an adult with disabilities was physically and mentally able to perform menial or what were called "mechanical" tasks such as peeling potatoes or sweeping floors, it wasn't enough to justify keeping them alive.[38]

Like the children before them, these men and women with special needs were collected from various institutions, boarded on buses, and brought to the killing centers. The staff at the facilities processed them as any other new patient, mainly to assure the patients and their families that nothing was out of the ordinary. The unsuspecting patients were led to believe the sudden change was just a routine transfer. They were then examined by doctors, which unbeknown to the individual was merely a means to gather information to falsify a realistic cause of death.[39]

Relatives and guardians of these deceased individuals were given falsified death certificates that listed natural causes like heart attack, pneumonia, stroke, or tuberculosis.[40] The pre-murder assessment was necessary to avoid red flags—for instance, listing a patient's death as appendicitis if they already had a scar, evidencing that their appendix had been taken out.[41] After the exam, patients undressed. Naked, they were led into a gas chamber that looked like a shower room. The door was shut and the gas released.

Before entering the killing room, some of the patients with disabilities were under the impression they were preparing to bathe and so entered willingly.[42] Others were less cooperative and had to be either sedated or forced inside. Some were tricked into the room under the false impression they would receive clothing.[43] At least one female patient somehow knew from the outset the horrible reality of what was to happen. While boarding the bus headed for the center, she cried out, "Is it my fault that I am born this way, and that they do this to me?"[44]

Dr. Albert Widmann, a chemist who was asked to obtain the carbon monoxide for these chemical showers, was once questioned if it was used to kill people. His chilling reply: "No. Animals in the form of humans."[45]

In total, at least 275,000 children and adults with special needs were killed, including those with mental impairment and nongenetic physical disabilities (such as veterans of World War I who had lost a limb) and people who were deaf and had behavioral problems.[46] This number, however, is a conservative estimate. It excludes those who were both Jewish and disabled, individuals with disabilities killed in occupied countries, and those who were murdered after the so-called end of the program. Accounting for these people, the actual number of children, men, and women with disabilities who were sterilized, exploited, or killed may realistically be as high as one million.[47]

DESECRATING THE IMAGE OF GOD

Thank you for sticking with me and reading this chapter. It is part of why it is so important that we don't look away from these painful, dark things but instead realize just how precious *every life* is. How worth fighting for. How can we do that without a careful, honest look at how quick the world can be to exploit and extinguish the lives of the vulnerable? Just by becoming aware—by looking again at what many people turn away from—you are taking the first step to change things.

> By becoming aware—by looking again at what many people turn away from—you are taking the first step to change things.

This history is not unique. I could fill an entire book with devastating stories of people who were victimized by both flawed systems and destructive ways of thinking. Hitler understood and used the term *image of God* to fit his agenda, his experiences, and his prejudices. In his mind, God's image fit a specific mold—and excluded anything that didn't.

It breaks my heart to know how many lives have never had a chance to truly experience the fullness of being made in God's image. It makes my heart race. It causes my muscles to tense up. It triggers my emotions to run wild. It's a deep pain, knowing that so much misery and suffering were caused because we didn't recognize the image of God in one another.

It's easy to think *I'd never be part of that*, but I wonder how many of us—me included—have unknowingly supported ideas or conversations that devalue other people? Every time I fail to lift up someone who is hurting, to realize someone's potential, or to stand with someone who is trying to do the right thing, I'm missing what God has mapped of Himself in each human being. This convicts me every day to be intentional, to see God's image in others and call it out. To help us all look again at *everyone* around us.

> Every time I fail to lift up someone who is hurting, to realize someone's potential, or to stand with someone who is trying to do the right thing, I'm missing what God has mapped of Himself in each human being.

People with disabilities make up the largest yet most overlooked and underserved population on earth. But Jesus' life tells a different story. More than 70 percent of His recorded miracles were for the most vulnerable population (the poor, widowed, oppressed, and people with disabilities, diseases, and illnesses). Sixty percent were for those who were "afflicted"—in today's language, those with special needs. Jesus' acts toward the forgotten and less-than in His time reveal His heart, a heart we're called to emulate. While we've made great strides in supporting people with disabilities, there's still a long way to go.

It's easy to value people who look like us, who move in our circles, who parrot our ideologies. But when I reflect on my own sinful and broken nature, I'm reminded to look deeper—not for sameness or for what we may have in common but for the worth God has placed in each person created in His image. Society may overlook them, but they're more than enough in God's eyes. And they should be in ours too.

The mini history lesson we've walked through is dramatic, raw, and uncomfortably real. It probably stirs up some emotion—and it should! Stories like these force us to confront the darkness and admit painful realities; they should also inspire us to care enough to act. When we witness suffering—like people being marginalized, abused, and exploited—it impacts our hearts deep within, igniting a sense that *this isn't right*. But why isn't it right? It's because we recognize something in them: a worth that demands acknowledgment. And that answer has everything to do with how we see ourselves and others and really with who we are.

Think back to the beginning of this chapter when I stood in the Olympic Stadium in 2023, a place once overshadowed by darkness and unspeakable injustice. If God were a Marvel superhero, redemption would be His defining power. To stand where crowds once cheered a leader who devalued and destroyed millions and now hear the roar of celebration for athletes with special needs was overwhelming. In that moment, I was struck with deep gratitude for a God who sees infinite value in every single life—and who writes stories of beauty in the very places that once bore so much pain.

This paints the perfect picture to illustrate the meaning of *renew*: "to flourish once more . . . to help someone flourish . . . to begin again."[48] That stadium, like the T4 program, was created for something terrible, something designed to devalue and discard lives. But now? Now it's a place filled with joy, celebration, and honor. What man intended for evil, God has reclaimed for His glory. Let this picture remind you that darkness doesn't get the final word. The gospel didn't end at the cross. Resurrection lies at the heart of our faith. Death was defeated, and hope rose in its place.

Hope changes our lens. It redefines how we view struggle, how we see ourselves, and how we treat the people around us. As we move forward, keep your heart open. Recognize the tension between the brokenness of the world and the unshakable truth that every human life is intentionally designed by God with inherent

> Resurrection lies at the heart of our faith.

worth and value. Yes, that includes *you*! If this is hard to believe about yourself, keep reading.

It's time to see others as they really are. It's time to recognize your worth too.

It's time to look again.

Chapter 2

IMAGE IS EVERYTHING

THREE SIMPLE WORDS ON A VINYL BUMPER STICKER forever changed the way I saw not just people with special needs but every human being ever created.

In 2021, our foundation marked the seventh Night to Shine (NTS) event, a worldwide celebration for individuals with special needs. A bit of history to frame things. Each NTS welcomes guests with all kinds of special (physical and neurological) needs. Some have Down syndrome, cerebral palsy, or autism, while others live with chronic illnesses like cystic fibrosis or epilepsy. Severe impairments such as spinal deformities, cleft palates, and craniofacial differences are also common. There are no limits at NTS—everyone with special needs and disabilities is welcome.

In Western society, people with special needs are often ignored or hidden from the world; in other countries, they face harsher realities. Considered cursed by evil spirits or seen as bad luck, many babies with special needs are abandoned in rivers or left for dead in dumpsters. Yes, this actually happens, and more often than you think.

Just look at how one of the NTS guests was treated in his hometown.

His mother shared, "I had lost hope. . . . One of the communities had advised me to strangle and suffocate him to death."

We at the foundation are doing everything to fight against these atrocious realities and at NTS do our best to treat our guests like the VIPs they are. When a parent sees their son or daughter cherished and celebrated for the first time, something shifts in their heart. We've seen that same shift happen in church leaders and even government officials, changing how entire communities perceive people with disabilities.

When we planned the details of our first NTS, we spent a lot of time—maybe too much time—picking the perfect annual date. We considered a slew of factors—weather, seasons, and significance, the perfect time for people to come together. Ultimately, we chose the Friday before Valentine's Day, a known holiday in the United States and many countries around the world that's focused on romantic love and self-indulgence. We wanted to flip the focus around to highlight God's love and the importance of choosing to love other people over ourselves.

At NTS, thousands of volunteers from local churches and communities in more than sixty countries line a red carpet, cheering as loud as they can and with thundering applause for each guest who steps onto it. The goal is to get to as many countries and to as many people as possible around the world. The itinerary of every NTS is adapted to fit each culture and context. There may be formal dinners or boxed lunches. Guests may enjoy karaoke and limo rides or tons of dancing and glow sticks. Still, whether in Guatemala City, Manila, or Charlotte, the vibe stays the same—God's love is lavished on every guest.

Aside from cheering their arrival on a red carpet, what happens toward the end of the evening is one of my favorite parts. In a special crowning ceremony, volunteers place a tiara or crown on the head of each guest, making them king or queen of NTS.

I believe NTS is a mere glimpse of the worth and love God lavishes on each one of our guests. I'm so grateful for our team and all the churches, partners, and volunteers that make this magical night a reality. A day or two after NTS, as we start planning the next one, I always hear the words from a mother who was at our very first event: "My daughter will never get married or have children, but tonight she will feel like a princess." This simultaneously heart-wrenching and hopeful phrase continually inspires me and the team to make each NTS even better than the last.

Over the years, we've received thousands of emails, letters, and text messages from host churches, guests, and parents of guests telling us why this night is so special. One church in Ukraine told us about a little boy whose alcoholic father had hung him by a hook on a wall. Suffering spine and nerve damage, he has trouble walking and controlling his body movements. The victim of constant bullying, this boy had a different experience at NTS. "For Egor to walk out on the red carpet . . . was such a big event. He . . . just felt so accepted and loved."

A church we partnered with in Kampala, Uganda, said, "Many people with physical disabilities in Uganda are abandoned by their families . . . They are kept behind doors and never allowed to speak and talk in public."

One mom told us that it was always difficult to hear people call her son "crazy," but that night she had tears in her eyes when she heard her son being called *rey* ("king" in Spanish).

Another mom said, "For this one night of the year, it doesn't matter one bit that she [my daughter] is differently abled. It doesn't matter that she has no concept of time, that she has short-term memory loss and literally behaves much like the Disney character Dory . . . It doesn't matter that she isn't capable of working a full-time job or going to college. It *does*, however, matter that she is a child of the one true King and that He has deemed her *worthy* of a purpose. It matters that she is loved by Him."

Another guest noted, "There are so many days we feel alone and forgotten. You made us feel like royalty." With stories like these, it's been incredible to witness how NTS has sparked transformation in individuals and across many communities.

BUMPER STICKER BREAKTHROUGH

Back to NTS 2021. Instead of the usual red carpet welcome, celebrations looked different depending on location. Some celebrated via video stream in the privacy of their homes, while others attended a drive-through version—these changes were made with safety in mind due to COVID-related realities. As ribbons of fiery red and orange stretched along the horizon that evening in Tucson, Arizona, I watched our honored guests wave from cars and SUVs that slowly inched down an imaginary version of a red carpet. As I always do, I cheered so loud I may have blasted the eardrums of the person standing beside me. Call me arrogant, but I like to think I win the prize for cheering our guests with the most passion.

Then, the red convertible crawled past. A young lady wearing a red dress stood in the back seat. A radiant smile lit up her face. In a rare moment, my mouth opened but no sound came out. My cheering got stuck somewhere between my chest and my throat. Time stopped as God drew my attention to the sticker on the bumper of the red convertible.

It read: Royalty on Board.

Suddenly, all I could hear was the rhythmic pounding of my heart.

To the best of my discernment, God seemed to whisper, *Don't miss this. I'm trying to show you something about My love for humanity. Don't miss this.*

"That's it!" I said out loud.

The revelation landed sharp and unexpectedly. *Royalty on Board* was the best way to describe the scene around me. For all the guests who have been shamed, ridiculed, or abandoned, the truth is that they are royalty in God's eyes—and not just one night of the year. NTS isn't a costume party where our guests remove how God sees them when they return home. They're still royalty wherever they go after NTS. They were royalty right from the beginning. They were royalty when the extra chromosome appeared on the amniocentesis, when the missing limb showed on the ultrasound, and when doctors said they would never walk or talk.

Since the inception of NTS, we've woven royal language into the making and marketing of the event. But for the first time, thinking of all the men and women, boys and girls we celebrate on this night, I had a sense that this language came from something deeper than the kings and queens we know of today. And it did!

Over the next several years, with the help of my team and later confirmed by several brilliant scholars, we discovered something that shocked me. The revelation I'm going to share with you, inspired by that two-by-two bumper sticker, wasn't just about NTS, it had everything to do with every human being ever created.

IMAGE *IS* EVERYTHING

Your image matters, but not in the way you might think.

In today's world, our public image—how we're perceived to the outside world—can feel like the ultimate difference-maker. It determines whether we land the job, secure the sponsorship, or gain the likes, the accolades, or the compliments. Many of us go to great lengths to polish and protect this image (especially the one we project online).

> Your image matters, but not in the way you might think.

And yet there's one perspective that shatters this illusion of worth—the perspective of the Creator, who sees and values every living being far more than any image we could ever project. To understand and truly grasp the full extent of what this means, let me take you back to the beginning of the Bible, where the story of human life as recorded in Scripture begins. I spent the first thirty-six years of my life missing something essential. Now I understand what it truly means to see ourselves and others and live the way He intended. I hope this truth is shared and preached more because I went so long without seeing it. And now that I understand, I can't unsee it.

Genesis 1 frames the divine-human relationship. Verses 26–27 describe God's final creation on the sixth day: humans. Dr. Catherine McDowell, Harvard grad and professor of classical Hebrew and ancient Near Eastern history, wrote that these key verses bear "pride of place being part of the opening chapter of God's written self-revelation."[1] Let's take a look.

> Then God said, "Let us make mankind *in our image*, in our likeness, so that they may rule over the fish in the sea and the birds in the sky, over the livestock and all the wild animals, and over all the creatures that move along the ground." So God created mankind *in his own image*, in the *image of God* he created them; male and female he created them.

If you've been in church, you've probably read or heard this scripture many times. Arguably, it might be almost as famous as Psalm 23 ("The LORD is my shepherd..."). These verses tell us that humans—all humans—were created in the "image of God" (*imago Dei* in Latin). In fact, they offer the very first mention of the word *image* in the Bible. Long before *image* became entangled with job titles, body size, social media presence, or financial status, it was meant to convey our true essence as a human being.

Genesis 1:26–27 presents humanity as created in God's image and likeness. As humans, we are unique, set apart from animals and all other living organisms. You can say we are the crown of creation. But what exactly does "image of God" mean and why does this matter?

Hitler had his own idea when he referred to "images of the Lord." Although the phrase he wrote in *Mein Kampf* invokes what you might think is a biblical slant, Hitler twisted religious language to fit his own idea of a divine ideal, which was to him the Aryan race. Clearly, his take on the "image of God" had nothing to do with its original meaning.

Throughout history, the phrase "image of God" has shaped many views on the divine-human relationship, sparking debate about its meaning among scholars, theologians, pastors, and laypeople for more than two millennia.[2]

THE BIG THREE

Out of over twenty interpretations, three major views have emerged that suggest the "image of God" in Genesis refers to the unique qualities that set humans apart from animals—specifically, three distinct abilities:

- Rational
- Relational
- Functional

RATIONAL. This view[3] highlights our inherent psychological makeup, spiritual nature, thought, rationale, intelligence, and emotion. Unlike your fur baby or giraffes in the open savanna of Africa, human beings have the capacity to reason and make moral decisions. We know right from wrong. We can solve complex problems, develop mathematical theories, and create technology, art, music, and literature.

RELATIONAL. This view emphasizes our ability to relate and grow with one another. It suggests that being made in God's image has to do with our connection with God and, by extension, with other people. This idea draws from the Christian concept of the Trinity, where God exists as three distinct yet unified persons: Father, Son, and Holy Spirit. Their perfect harmony serves as a model for human relationships as "male *and* female" (Genesis 1:27). As the Trinity exists in perfect relationship, God made humankind, both "male and female," to reflect His unity. Our primary relationship is with God, and through this we build meaningful relationships with others. We have and make friends. We work to build harmony with one another and contribute to society. We can enter into deep relationships with God and other people on a level animals cannot.

FUNCTIONAL. This perspective holds that humans differ from animals and reflect God's likeness through our responsibility to steward His creation and serve as His representatives on earth. This view is not based on human biology or relationships but on the authority we hold and how we use it. It's influenced by the biblical mandate to "*rule* over the fish in the sea and the birds in the sky, over the livestock and all the wild animals, and over all the creatures that move along the ground" (Genesis 1:26) and "Be fruitful and increase in number; fill the earth and subdue it. *Rule* over the fish in the sea and the birds in the sky and over every living creature that moves on the ground" (Genesis 1:28). Unlike animals, we can manage, steward, and creatively engage with the world around us. We care for the environment. We build societies with intricate systems of governance, law, and education. According to this view, being made in God's image involves actively participating in and contributing to the world in meaningful ways. The functional position of the "image of God" gets the most press for obvious reasons. It's about what humans can *do*.

SOMETHING'S MISSING

Though these views are distinct, they have one thing in common: They associate "image of God" with a particular trait or ability that human beings have. Though each school of thought holds merit, a problem remains. Each category excludes some of the most vulnerable populations. This can't be the whole story.

What about people who have physical, mental, or developmental disabilities? Does a human being with a genetic impairment or autism reflect less of God's image because his or her rational, relational, or functional capacities are limited or absent?

Does Alfredito, my twenty-two-year-old friend from Guatemala who has never been invited to a birthday party because he has Down syndrome, somehow fall short of God's image? What about the child with the terminal illness who is neurologically impaired and has spent her life hooked up to machines? She can't express her level of pain to her doctors, but is she made less in God's likeness because she can't lead a movement? Hitler's regime would have thought so. But that conclusion can't be right; it doesn't reflect the Father's heart as revealed in the Bible.

So back to the perplexing question, What exactly does "image of God" mean?

Chapter 3

THE TRUTH OF WHO WE ARE

ONE OF MY FAVORITE STORIES IN THE BIBLE IS about a young man who became crippled when he was five years old. Mephibosheth (*meh-fib'-o-sheth*) was the son of Jonathan, who was the son of King Saul. Mephibosheth's future was bright as an heir to the throne of Israel. Things soured when King Saul and Jonathan were killed. Back at the palace, when the little boy's nanny found out the devastating news, chaos ensued.

In that time in history, the fall of a kingdom's ruler often meant a death sentence for his entire family. The lineage had to be wiped out to prevent any chance of rallying a revolt or challenging the new leadership's claim to power. Knowing this, Mephibosheth's nanny's maternal instinct kicked in—protect and run. She snatched the boy and fled. In her haste, however, she accidentally dropped him; or the boy may have tripped and fallen on his own—we don't know exactly which. Regardless, the seemingly tragic outcome remained the same: Mephibosheth became crippled for life (2 Samuel 4:4).

The etymology of this little boy's name is interesting: "blown out of shame."[1] I'm also fascinated by where he came to live, a village called Lo Debar, which meant "no pasture," a place nicknamed "nothing."[2] Once an heir to a royal throne, this five-year-old kid started a new life at a severe disadvantage, a stranger with a disability living in "Nothing Town."[3] To most outsiders, this is a picture of a meaningless, tragic life. In ancient biblical times, disabilities were often seen as a source of shame. Many believed physical and other limitations were linked to divine punishment.[4] As a result, people with disabilities were marginalized from society and restricted from participating in religious life.

THROUGH THE EYES OF A KING

Scholars believe Mephibosheth was either a teenager or young adult when he encountered the new king of Israel, David, King Saul's nemesis. One day, as King David remembered his late best friend, Jonathan, he asked his servant, "Is there anyone still left of the house of Saul, so that I could show him kindness for Jonathan's sake?" (2 Samuel 9:1 NASB). At first glance, it might seem that King David had become suspicious after being hunted by King Saul in the wilderness. Was there a potential coup in the making?

Mephibosheth, the only living reminder of the king's greatest friendship, came before the throne. The rush of nostalgia and tender emotion likely brought tears to David's eyes, while Mephibosheth was probably trembling in his dusty sandals.

"Do not be afraid," David began, perhaps seeing a flash of the boy's father in his eyes, "for I will assuredly show kindness to you for the sake of your father Jonathan, and I will restore to you all the land of your grandfather Saul; and you yourself shall eat at my table regularly" (2 Samuel 9:7 NASB). Mephibosheth's response reflected the depth of his wrecked self-image. "What is your servant, that you should be concerned about a dead dog like me?" (v. 8 NASB). A dead dog not only has no worth; it is also vile. But that's not what the king saw.

David recognized a man who had innate worth and invited him to sit at the table of royalty for the rest of his life. David saw value when no one else did. Just as this ancient earthly king recognized worth in someone who saw himself as worthless, God sees you as infinitely valuable, even if you don't. Sometimes you need a king to tell you who you are.

> Sometimes you need a king to tell you who you are.

But I'm getting ahead of myself.

Despite the prejudice society may have had, the Bible promotes compassion and kindness toward people with disabilities. These ideas are woven throughout Scripture. Mephibosheth is not the only recipient of this inclusion. Take Moses. When God first called him to lead Israel out of Egypt, Moses balked. He refused to step up, blaming his speech impediment.[5] We may not know the full extent of Moses' struggle, but it was enough to keep him out of the ring, at least in his eyes. Whether it was poor oral skills, a prominent lisp, or a severe stutter, God wasn't fazed by what shattered Moses' confidence. In fact, He doubled down. He reassured Moses by affirming His sovereignty and omnipotence. It's as if God was saying, "Moses, you can do what I'm calling you to do because it has less to do with you and more to do with Me." God's power plus our willingness equals an unstoppable team!

> God's power plus our willingness equals an unstoppable team!

The New Testament is also filled with encounters between Jesus and people with disabilities. In every instance, He comes close. He sees them. He calls them by name. These actions emphasize their worth and dignity.

If you consider the high value with which people with neurological or physical differences are treated throughout the Bible, the three frameworks (rational, relational, and functional) seem incomplete. They don't fully connect to or reveal the heart of God.

This led me to ask: Could there be a more probable explanation for what our God-given "image" means? Yes! Turns out, many scholars, including Michael Bird, Carmen Imes, J. Richard Middleton, and Catherine McDowell, scripturally, theologically, and historically have confirmed my initial convictions.

A ROYAL IMPLICATION

The key to deeper understanding starts with the Hebrew words for "image" (*tselem*) and "likeness" (*demuth*) used in Genesis 1:26–27 to introduce the first humans.[6] In short, scholars have said *tselem* is primarily a term used in the Old Testament to refer to a statue or idol, while *demuth* is more abstract but usually has to do with visual similarity.[7] So, is Genesis saying we're God's idol or statue? Well, not quite.

In ancient cultures like Egypt and Assyria, kings were often called the "image" of their god, meaning they were seen as the visible representatives of divine rule on earth. But Genesis flips the script—those same words used for kings are now applied to all people.

That means every human being carries royal worth, not just the powerful or elite. Let that sink in for a moment. Could the "image of God" really have a royal implication for all human life? Many experts in Old Testament and ancient Near East studies I've talked to believe so. I've even been told that among these scholars, the "royalty view" is likely the most accurate view.

It's no coincidence that Adam was given the task of caring for the garden of Eden. Gardening back in those days was fit for a king, quite literally. Mesopotamian history teaches us that kings were known for acquiring rare trees and plants from lands they conquered, bringing them back to their gardens, and making them flourish.[8] When you stop to think about it, Adam wasn't just tending to a garden, he was living out his royal identity.

As I began to unpack this "royalty view," I learned that the biblical text goes one step further.

GOD'S VALUE STATEMENT

A few chapters down in Genesis 5, we find the only other place in the Bible where image and likeness are linked together:[9] "When Adam had lived 130 years, he had a son in his own likeness, in his own image; and he named him Seth" (Genesis 5:3). Just as Seth belonged to Adam's family, God's intention was for humans to belong to His. So, being made in God's image isn't just about royal worth; it's also about belonging. In short, being made in God's image means we're not just valuable—we're family. And that truth changes everything.

> Being made in God's image isn't just about royal worth; it's also about belonging.

When you zoom out, it's incredible—the phrase "image of God" isn't rooted in what we do, how smart we are, or how we relate to one another. It's ultimately a declaration of value, a royal and familial identity given by God Himself.

Like Mephibosheth, sometimes you need a king to tell you who you are. And the King of kings says: *You are Mine. You matter. You are My royal image.*

That's not just a title; it's a value statement. A worth statement. A royal and family statement that stretches across all human history.

Out of everything God made, only humans were given that kind of dignity. Such a simple phrase gives us a glimpse into the heart of God. He simply made us with royal worth and desires to be in relationship with us. The biblical author isn't whispering that truth . . . he's declaring it!

Imagine as an ancient Israelite hearing Genesis 1 being read for the first time thousands of years ago. The story you've heard growing up is the same—surrounding nations boast that their king is the image of their pagan god. The most powerful, the most elite, the ones with status and strength are chosen to represent the divine. Exclusivity at its finest. Everyone else? Ordinary. Left out. But then Moses or another Israelite leader stands tall, reading aloud the Creation story as part of the law and covenant given by God. Proclaiming the Word of Yahweh, the one and only true God, he describes the formation of the universe. Then he gets to day 6—*and God created mankind in His image.* I can almost see the crowd, eyes narrowing, some tilting their heads. *What did you say again, Moses? Image of . . . ? I know that term! It's a term meant for a king!*

Imagine being hit in that moment with the sacred and revolutionary truth that you, your mother, your sibling, the person standing in front of and behind you were made in the image of the one true King, that you all have royal worth. Wow! This news would have taken their breath away. It still takes my breath away today.

Recently at a speaking event, I was approached by a woman who has a son with disabilities. Her face lit up when she shifted the conversation to her son who had attended that year's NTS. Her voice was full of joy as she shared how much it had meant to him. "My son really believes he's a king on that night," she said with a little laugh, clearly moved.

"Well, he is!" I responded. Then I leaned in and said, "And he's a king not just on that night. In God's eyes, he is a king every day, always."

It was a simple exchange but a profound reminder that just like this woman's son, we have royal worth, not just on a spotlighted night, but always.

INFINITE VALUE—WOMB TO TOMB

Let's take this same truth and make it personal. At the very beginning of Scripture, on the very first page that lays the foundation for all human history, God declares infinite value and worth over you, me, and everyone else—womb to tomb! Catherine McDowell said it like this: "Humans are endowed with the royal status because they are made in the image and likeness of God."[10]

It's mindboggling how long it took me to connect the dots. "Royalty on Board" was not just an impactful bumper sticker, it signified a timeless, biblical truth. A number of words come to mind when I think about royalty: *power, honor, nobility, legacy, identity, belonging, prestige, the best of the best, inheritance, authority.* What comes to mind for you? There's something about the word *royalty* that sends a spark to our hearts. It carries a certain weight and aura.

Many of us around the world, particularly those who are governed by monarchs, are glued to every move, every headline, and every scandal because we're obsessed with status and influence.

We're drawn to the mystique of royal bloodlines, the pageantry of coronations, and the notion of legacy. We watch fictional movies and documentaries about kings and queens because deep down we hope to live a life that is seen, valued, and celebrated. We even call little girls princesses because it's one of the simplest ways to tell them they are loved and cherished. Demi and I chose the middle name Reign for our daughter Daphne to remind her that she is deeply precious and truly treasured.

> Our intrinsic worth as *royalty* is a hint that we were designed for more.

Our intrinsic worth as *royalty* is a hint that we were designed for more. Not for a kingdom of this world that can be conquered or fade from history but for a kingdom that is eternal. A kingdom that invites every single person, not only those with a family crest, to be a part of it.

NO OPTING OUT OF WORTH

This royal reality affirms the value of people that society has written off. It offers intrinsic worth to the men and women with disabilities who spend their lives confined within the four walls of institutions, never seeing the light of day . . . to the children stuck in bed or wheelchairs, who in the eyes of the world have nothing to contribute . . . to the boy left in a wine barrel, his body deformed for life . . . to the girl whose mother boiled her eye out just to earn more as a beggar. These individuals are royalty—not just in the eyes of advocates but in the eyes of the God who created them. They are worth more than they know.

Has anyone told them?

Has anyone told *you*?

Here's the thing. You can reject a lot of things in life. You can reject help. You can reject forgiveness. You can even reject the gospel itself. But here's what you can't reject: You can't reject the fact that you were made in the image of God. You can ignore it. You can run from it. But you can't erase it.

Your worth doesn't come from what you do, what you've done, or what's been done to you. It comes from who made you. And that's the part you can't undo. No matter how deep your wounds go or how many regrets you carry, your status as God's royal image stands firm. God's fingerprints are all over you.

> You can't reject the fact that you were made in the image of God.

That's what makes this reality life-changing. The world may have written off those men and women in the institutions. It may have cast aside the boy in the barrel and the girl in the streets. But God hasn't. Not for a second. His image is still on them. And it's still on you.

Our royal reality means that everyone has dignity and value. Stop and think about that. Every. Single. Person. The one you love to praise and the one you belittle under your breath. A complete stranger. The family member with whom you hold opposite political views. The guilty prisoner sentenced to a life behind bars. The person you're inspired by and the person who has hurt you in unspeakable ways. They are all royalty to God.

Do those last sentences make you cringe? Maybe you pictured someone who hurt you deeply. Someone whose face you'd rather forget. I don't say this lightly. I know how painful that can be. But here's what's true: No matter what they've done—and no matter what you've done—none of it can change the fact that God made us in His image. That truth doesn't bend or break based on our choices.

You can reject the gospel. But you can't reject your worth.

Let's focus in more closely. If you've been battered by self-criticism or bruised by the hands or words of others, you may struggle with accepting this royal reality. I don't know your story, but I'd love to share a glimpse of mine and how I wrestled with my self-image.

Chapter 4

OUR ROYAL REALITY

ON A SUMMER DAY IN 2021, I FACED THE MEN WHO would determine my athletic future. The AC hit my face with an icy blast. It couldn't have been more than seventy degrees in that room, but my palms couldn't stop sweating. A few weeks earlier, I was on the brink of signing with the Jacksonville Jaguars. Even better than the prospect of getting to wear a football jersey again was the chance to play for my old college coach. Talk about a blessing in the making. If this winding journey—bouncing from a handful of football teams to swinging a bat with the New York Mets in the minors, and then back to the NFL—was God's way of bringing my passion for football to life, then count me in all the way!

Except it wasn't.

Sitting in the office at the Jags facility, my ears tuned into the flood of compliments, explanations, and extra words meant to dull the edge. The bottom line? I was cut. Fired from the team. Again. If you're not familiar with my sports journey, the Jags was the fourth NFL team that let me go from their roster since getting traded from the Denver Broncos to the New York Jets in 2012. You could say that déjà vu has a sense of humor, one I wasn't feeling at the time.

This conversation with Coach Meyer and the general manager happened a day or two after my thirty-fourth birthday. I'm not the kind of guy who celebrates their anniversary of existence all month long, but the rejection from this NFL team stung just a little bit more.

When I got home, Demi was waiting for me with kind words and open arms. Even with her sweet support, the setback unsettled me. It didn't help that running nonstop on almost every sports channel and on social media were clips of all my worst plays from the one and only preseason game I played with the Jags. Subconsciously, I threw all these questions at myself—none of which had a good answer.

Did I really just give up baseball for getting cut at football?

Is this going to be my last chance ever at sports?

Is this what defines all my years of grinding?

What are people going to think or say?

When I was released from the New England Patriots in 2013, it was truly gut-wrenching. But this experience hit differently. I can't say reliving this moment with you makes me excited, but it's a reminder of how our self-image can change in an instant.

More than anything, I was embarrassed. The mirror through which I looked at myself was cloudy. I'd studied the concept of identity enough—I'd even written a book on it—to know that grounding yourself in external circumstances can mess with the truth of who you really are. The combination of being cut and the noise of outside voices did not make me question my identity in God, but looking back it definitely brought me to a low point internally.

Based on the downward spiral of a single conversation, I felt a similar plunge in the joy I once took in life's simplest pleasures— like spending time with my wife; climbing into bed with Chunk, my Bernese Mountain dog, and my other two fur babies; and lifting someone's spirits in a chance encounter. My spirit and outlook fell flat.

With all the negativity swirling in my head, I couldn't help but think of one thing: *myself*! It was *my image* on the line. My pride. My legacy. My this. My that. The viewfinder I was using to frame my life? *Me!*

Maybe you can relate? Image is everything, right? There's some truth to that maxim. Image, particularly our self-image, has a way of seeping into our thoughts and actions, subtly shaping what we believe about who we are and contradicting the truth of who we actually are.

It's no secret that a poor self-image can lead us down a dark tunnel of despair.

THE WEIGHT OF A LOW SELF-IMAGE

I received a letter from a sophomore student at Harvard University sharing his struggles as an incoming freshman. He told me how students who first arrive on campus think of themselves much like the lead actor in their own school play. These are valedictorians, team captains, and prodigies. The campus is packed with people who have been told they are "the best." But something happens when you step onto the bigger stage of an Ivy League university. It's like being in a pressure cooker. Some students will rise to the occasion, but for many others, according to this student, their once intact sense of self crumbles. He put it like this:

> Harvard breaks people. For the first time, our exceptionalism isn't enough. More than half of all Harvard students experience symptoms of depression during their four years. Other students often struggle finding their true purpose in an environment of vanity. Around me, students who had defined themselves by their past achievements were floundering. Some turned to partying, others to campus mental health services. Tragically, too many lost their lives

to suicide. The unrelenting pressure to succeed left many questioning their purpose and identity.

This student was all too familiar with this feeling. Hailing from a lineage of Harvard graduates and star lacrosse players, he hoped to continue the legacy. Despite hard work, however, injuries sidelined his dreams. In the wake of shattered expectations, this young man was forced to face an internal crisis, ultimately realizing that his identity wasn't tied to sports, grades, or social status but to his faith in Jesus Christ. Unfortunately, this isn't the case for everyone. In his words, "For so many students, their thirst for love, meaning, and purpose goes unquenched."

You don't need to attend an Ivy League college to struggle with understanding who you are. Our world is facing an image problem, evidenced by skyrocketing incidences of depression, loneliness, and low self-esteem. Take depression, a common but serious mood disorder that affects all aspects of a person's life, such as sleeping, eating, and socializing. There are different forms of depression, and some are more severe than others. In the United States alone, 29 percent (one-third) of adults have reported being diagnosed with depression. That's a big jump—nearly 10 percentage points—since 2015.[1] And that doesn't even factor in the people who suffer in silence.

Depression isn't something that happens only in Western society. Around the world, nearly four in ten adults, fifteen and older, struggle with it or know someone close who does.[2] In one study on mental health, young adults used the following words to describe themselves:[3]

"Embarrassed."
"Inept."
"Clueless."

"Inferior."
"Worthless."

Have you ever felt any of these ways about yourself?

So many things contribute to depression—stress, medical issues, trauma, life transitions. The list is endless. Our modern way of living, thanks to less movement and more screen time, certainly isn't helping. One of the biggest culprits? A lack of purpose. A recent study found roughly three out of five young adults (or 58 percent) experienced hopelessness from a "lack of meaning and purpose."[4] The same study reported that half of the people surveyed also struggled with a "lack of direction" in their lives. In the absence of purpose, depression and anxiety grows. It's almost impossible to see a way out of lingering or suffocating darkness. While it's shocking, it's not surprising that suicide is the third leading cause of death of people between the ages of fifteen and twenty-nine.[5]

So, why am I sharing all this? A lack of meaning can embed itself so deeply in our self-image that it blinds us from our royal worth, the truth of who we are. And what a tragedy that would be!

THE REAL MASTERPIECE

Recently, Demi and I visited the Rijksmuseum, a famous art museum featuring masterpieces from great Dutch artists like Vermeer, Rembrandt, and Van Gogh. The place was packed. While I'm definitely not an art connoisseur—I'm more of a people person than a painting guy—Demi's heart was set on seeing one-of-a-kind masterpieces, worth millions, that have shaped history and preserved the memories of artists long gone. Speaking of millions, in 2023 the Rijksmuseum acquired Rembrandt's

The Standard Bearer for 175 million euros ($191.3 million).[6] And that's just one out of thousands of paintings in this museum. Talk about value!

I remember standing in front of one painting in particular. At least thirty art lovers stood locked in time, admiring the brushstrokes of the work or the history behind it or marveling at the artist's technique. Many were holding up their phones to capture a snapshot of the carefully preserved strokes of oil on a canvas.

Before I say what I'm about to say, I do not mean to diminish the beauty of art or the talent behind the artist; I may not understand art, but I know it takes something special to create something meaningful. As I watched the gawking and awestruck crowd, I realized something.

If they had flipped their phones to selfie mode, they would have seen a true masterpiece. They would have seen a living and breathing human being, designed by the Master architect of the universe. They would have seen a masterpiece that is infinitely more valuable than any multimillion-dollar painting. Because that's who we are. That's who you are, the pinnacle of creation made on purpose.

When we don't recognize or believe our true worth as God's masterful creation, we settle for hollow substitutes. We rely on the opinions of others, our social status, or our accomplishments to make us feel better and look good. We chase approval from others rather than focus on what matters most. We get stuck in a vicious cycle of self-doubt, anxiety, or stress when things don't turn out a certain way.

> When we don't recognize or believe our true worth as God's masterful creation, we settle for hollow substitutes.

All this can ultimately lead us in a direction that contrasts with what Jesus promised in John 10:10 was an "abundant" life. In fact, the Greek word John used for abundant, *perisson*, is much deeper and fuller than what you might define as abundant. *Perisson* describes a life "exceedingly, very highly, beyond measure, more, superfluous, a quantity so abundant as to be considerably more than what one would expect or anticipate."[7] I don't know about you, but that's the kind of life I want. And that's the kind of life God came to give.

I want to sit with you and explore the unique way you were created, so you can see yourself through God's eyes—not for what you've achieved or the praise you've earned, and not based on your failures or losses, but simply because you are human.

HUMANS, THE PINNACLE OF CREATION

Imagine having a puppy who curls up beside you as you settle in for the next episode of your favorite TV show. As you run your fingers through his silky fur, a content whimper escapes his lips. There's something undeniably special about the interaction, isn't there? Warm, fuzzy, and beautiful. Or those frosty mornings, when you step outside and pause for a few seconds, allowing the sun's golden warmth to kiss your face. Almost magical, right? Whether we consider the thought or sight of a beloved pet, a favorite place, or a stunning view that leaves us awestruck, there's one creation that stands uniquely apart—humans.

We are the pinnacle of creation. You and me. How do we know this? This truth is reflected in God's orchestration of creation in several ways. I'll highlight three of them.

Divine Discussion

Biblical scholars agree that God created the universe in a structured and intentional way. The process is traditionally

> We are the pinnacle of creation.

summed up in two words: *forming* and *filling*. Each stage, or day, builds on the previous one.

> Day 1: God divided light from darkness.
> Day 2: God created the sky.
> Day 3: God created the earth, sea, and vegetation (with food, fruits, and seeds).
> Day 4: God created the sun, moon, and stars.
> Day 5: God created birds and creatures of the sea.
> Day 6: God created land animals and humans.
> Day 7: God rested.

Days 1–3, God formed. He set the stage for life. Days 4–6, He filled. Living things occupied the spaces He had formed on the previous days. Note a significant change on day 6. The shift begins with the language that God used. During the previous five days, He launched each creative work with the following declaration: "Let there" or "Let the" (Genesis 1:3, 6, 9, 11, 14, 20, 24). Verse 26 breaks the pattern: "*Let us make* mankind in our image, in our likeness, so that they may rule over the fish in the sea and the birds in the sky, over the livestock and all the wild animals, and over all the creatures that move along the ground."

Did you notice the plural expression "Let *us* make"? If you're wondering who "us" is, scholars suggest it refers to the Trinity (Father God, Jesus the Son, and the Holy Spirit) or some type of heavenly audience (angelic beings). Nevertheless, it would seem quite fitting that the Trinity was present at the beginning of creation. So, what's the big deal with "us"?

What sets this verse—and its phrasing—apart from the other commands is that, unlike with the other creatures that were simply spoken into existence, God paused and deliberated before creating the first human beings. The expression "Let *us* make" underscores some sort of divine discussion.

God's Exhale

Another break in the creation pattern is that God formed Adam from the dust of the earth. And unlike animals and insects, God *breathed* life into him: "Then the LORD God formed a man from the dust of the ground and breathed into his nostrils the breath of life, and the man became a living being" (Genesis 2:7). No other living thing received the divine exhale of God Almighty!

This is one of the most intimate pictures of the relationship between God and humans. On the sixth day, the Creator of the universe came close. Leaning in from a backdrop of billions of galaxies, God sank His hand into the earth. Taking what could have been a fine powder or rich soil, He pressed and sculpted the dust into curves, lines, and nooks, filling hollow spaces with veins, tendons, and muscle. And then, God drew His breath. He covered the mouth of flesh and bone and set the air free, sparking the first inhale of humanity.

The way God made man signifies not just a making but a giving of Himself.[8] Though animals are remarkable creatures—and believe me, I'm biased toward dogs, especially my three fur babies at home—they were not crafted with the same level of intimacy. When human beings are formed into existence, God is personally involved.

According to God's Image

One more disruption in the creation rhythm is that up to that point, God made all living things that bark, hiss, roar, or moo "according to their kind."[9]

> The way God made man signifies not just a making but a giving of Himself.

Humans, however, were created to be like God, made in His image and likeness. The author of Genesis chose not to use "according to their kind" but instead chose to describe humanity as created according to God's "own image"—as God's *kind*! You may not see this as a big deal, but from a literary standpoint, the author is flashing a big neon sign that says This Is Too Important to Gloss Over! Although the ancient poetic pattern is often lost in translations, make no mistake, each original word in the Creation narrative is carefully crafted. Humankind is not just a "kind." We were made for *more*.

What conclusion can we draw from all this? Human beings matter to God in a way that no other creature ever could. As Paul Tripp wrote, "Adam and Eve are not just part of the catalog of creatures that God made. They are above, they are special, and they are christened with a dignity that separates them from everything else."[10] King David echoed this remarkable truth when he wrote Psalm 8:

> What is mankind that you are mindful of them,
>   human beings that you care for them?
>
> You have made them a little lower than the angels
>   and crowned them with glory and honor.
> You made them rulers over the works of your hands;
>   you put everything under their feet. (Psalm 8:4–6)

David marveled at the fact that God, the Creator of all things, not only considers humans but cares about them. Interestingly, this passage also foreshadows Jesus, the ultimate "image of God" to ever walk the earth.[11]

You and I are personal to God. We are ever present in the thought life of God. His actions breathe life into our story. Just thinking about this gives me chills—it's a humbling reminder. I often forget, or take for granted, that I was created with such love and intention.

IN, BY, FOR *LOVE*

I like to say we were made *in* Love, *by* Love, and *for* Love! Since God *is* Love, it seems fitting.

God created you *in* love. God didn't create us out of frustration, obligation, or indifference. He wasn't rushed. He wasn't distracted. Unlike how we sometimes put together furniture or an appliance and get irritated by confusing directions or how long it's taking, He made us with care and intention and completely deliberately.

God created you *by* love. God didn't pass off the task of our creation to an angel or another being. He designed us personally. His love was the driving force behind every detail. You and I are here as a direct result of His perfect and intentional love because that's who He is, Love (1 John 4:8).

God created you *for* love. We were made for a purpose that is centered on love—to be in a relationship with God and to reflect His love to others. At the core of our being, we were created to experience and enjoy God's love by walking in and sharing it with others. He desires you to spend eternity with Him, living in the fullness of the love He designed for you.

God made you exactly as you are, with a perfect plan for your life. You are not an accident, a rushed creation, or a product of imperfection—as an image of *the* King, you are royalty!

The scriptural truth of our uniqueness and being made "of God" serves as an equilibrium, a balance that keeps us from thinking too highly or too lowly of ourselves. As one scholar put it, "The image of

God motif hits the reset button"[12] for how we should see ourselves. We are not God, nor are we mere animals.

At our core, our identity depends on God. It's less about us and more about the One who created us.

You might be wondering, *How does sin play into all this?* I'm glad you asked! I'll get there in the next chapter, but for now know that while sin has created catastrophic problems for us as humans, it hasn't erased our image. Our identity, our worth, doesn't have to end with brokenness. God's plan is for us to be "conformed to the image of his Son" (Romans 8:29) who is the ultimate "image of the invisible God" (Colossians 1:15).

When I reflect on the royal status God has bestowed on every human being, I'm reminded of Cyndi and Kurt Petrich—a couple who went above and beyond to show their adopted daughters that they are, indeed, royalty.

ROYALTY ON BOARD

In May 2015, Cyndi and Kurt, a widow and a widower, went on a mission trip to Ukraine to serve orphans with special needs. Although they began the trip as strangers, by the time they headed home, they had fallen for each other. But beyond finding love again, they discovered a shared passion—serving orphans. Cyndi and Kurt eventually married and, with hearts open to God's leading, returned to Eastern Europe for several mission trips—ready to serve wherever He called them. On one trip, they met a four-year-old girl who would turn their lives upside down in the best way they could ever imagine.

Drowning in an oversized sweater, Dasha sat at a little table, her brown hair clipped into an uneven pixie cut. Though within earshot of giggles and squeals from a handful of other kids, it was obvious no one dared come close to Dasha. In fact, when one of the women in charge of the orphanage noticed the Petrichs' interest in the girl, she darted toward them. "Be careful," the woman warned the couple, "Dasha has HIV."

Dismissing the heads-up, the couple sat down with the little girl, who couldn't stop smiling. Cyndi and Kurt sensed something special about her. That night God began whispering to their hearts, separately, about the possibility of adopting Dasha. The little girl's face would appear in their dreams for many nights. The couple had no idea then, but a little more than three years later, they'd return to the orphanage—this time, to bring Dasha home with them for good.

Dasha's "gotcha" (adoption) day in September 2018 was planned to perfection. Inspired by the sight of a horse-drawn carriage in a nearby park, Cyndi and Kurt were struck with an idea. In Cyndi's words, "Leaving the orphanage was something we thought might be scary for Dasha, so we wanted to give her the most beautiful experience possible. We also wanted her to know how loved she was by us and her Father in heaven."

In addition to picking her up in a horse-drawn carriage, they brought her a lavender gown with a tulle skirt, sleeveless and airy, allowing for countless twirls. The dress was complete with white full-length gloves and topped with a sparkly tiara. Beyond a display of fashion or of kindness, Cyndi and Kurt sought to make clear to Dasha, as literally as possible, that she is the daughter of the King of kings and the Lord of lords. No longer abandoned, this little girl was royalty.

Swinging the door open to the orphanage to welcome Dasha into her new forever family is something the Petrichs will never forget. Her pixie cut had grown into shoulder-length pigtails by then. As she pranced around the room, they whipped around her face. Bubbling with excitement, Dasha repeatedly squealed, "Mama! Papa!" After swapping out her drab orphanage clothes for the lavender dress, gloves, and tiara, the family of three walked hand in hand out of the orphanage.

Cyndi counted down from ten until Dasha's feet hit the curb. And there, the rhythmic clip-clop of a horse's hooves echoed down the street. On the ride to their hotel, Kurt sat beside his daughter and held her hand. Cyndi encouraged her to wave at passersby like the princess she was. And both mom and dad reminded Dasha that although they loved her so much, it was God who sought after her. They whispered to her words they'd told her since the first day the three of them met. "He's seen you, Dasha. He's always seen you."

Dasha's gotcha day was bittersweet. While her dream of being adopted by a loving mom and dad came true, she left behind her best friend at the orphanage. Tanya, also diagnosed with HIV, was the only child Dasha was able to play with. The two girls were inseparable. Back in the United States, Dasha would pray in Ukrainian every day, "Please, God. Bring Tanya home." With their finances drained, Cyndi and Kurt didn't have the means to move forward with a second adoption. Their daughter's prayers looked hopeless.

In nothing short of a miracle, the Petrichs received a grant and immediately initiated the adoption process for Tanya. Upon informing the orphanage, there was a twist. Tanya had a sister named Veronica who was living in another orphanage at the time. The two sisters could not be adopted separately. Another twist—Veronica had cerebral palsy. Cyndi and Kurt found themselves in a foggy terrain. How would they care for a third child with even more severe special needs that demanded additional resources and medical attention?

Cyndi recalled sensing her heavenly Father's whisper in her heart: "You don't have to do this, but oh, if you do, it will be beautiful." With

God's assurance, the Petrichs moved forward to include two more beautiful girls into their family.

Cyndi and Kurt knew Tanya and Veronica's gotcha day would not be complete without fancy dresses and a horse-drawn carriage ride. As they put it, "God never misses an opportunity to show us how much He loves us and how perfect we are to Him; how could we not show the girls the same thing?"

For Cyndi, the act of dressing the girls in their new fancy clothes and adorning their heads with shiny tiaras carried deep significance. More than an act of care, it was a glimpse of God's love. It was a reminder that He strips away our old selves, clothes us in new royal robes, and welcomes us as His own.

As the sisters sat in the horse-drawn carriage, smiling and waving to the people who sat on benches or walked by, they knew in their hearts that they were special. Tanya and Veronica knew that good things were in store for them. And they knew that it was God who made all of it possible.

At the time of this writing, Cyndi and Kurt had traveled to Bulgaria to adopt their fourth daughter, Maria, who has significant neurological needs. Maria is severely intellectually delayed and non-verbal. Although the Petrichs understand those words are written on Maria's medical records, they also recognize that God doesn't define her by those terms. Maria is royalty, and yes, of course Kurt and Cyndi gave their daughter a royal experience on her gotcha day! Dasha. Tanya. Veronica. Maria. You. Me. Our royal reality was set long before I wrote this book. But the story doesn't stop there.

Chapter 5

WHEN ROYALTY GOES WRONG

AFTER GOD BREATHED LIFE INTO MAN, IT UNFORtunately didn't take long for a darker reality to emerge. In a garden, sin dismantled the perfect relationship between human and divine. Though paradise was choked by this three-letter word, God's plan for redemption was already taking shape. The chasm that separated us from a personal relationship with God would be bridged through one man, both fully human and fully divine. Redemption would come. Relationship would finally be restored.

Though not everyone would receive this gift of new life, the invitation would extend to all.

A WELCOME WITH NO LIMITS

Each year, about two million visitors around the world travel to the peak of Mount Corcovado. They don't ascend the twenty-three-hundred-plus-foot slope via a train, trolley, or van only to admire the mountain's unusual hunchback shape. Visitors come to marvel at the ninety-eight-foot reinforced concrete statue that rests at its peak—*Christ the Redeemer*, one of the New Seven Wonders of the World. If you've seen the fifth film in the *Fast and the Furious* series, you know what statue I'm talking about. It was why I was up at 3:30 a.m. during our visit to Brazil for an NTS event.

That morning, our team and some local pastors were blessed with a private tour of the statue before it opened to the public. I hopped in one of two vans for the winding, thirty-minute drive up the mountain. Armed with Dramamine and ginger chews, we thankfully avoided any puking incidences despite the seemingly never-ending loop of hairpin turns. It was too dark to see the Tijuca rainforest as we drove through it, and most of us had our eyes closed anyway, fighting nausea.

At 5:00 a.m., I stepped out of the elevator doors that opened at the base of the statue. A stream of grays streaked with blues swept around me. Toward my left, the soft glow of city lights waned as the tangerine sky spilled over the earth's edge. A glance upward caught a sliver of moon. I sucked in my breath. We hadn't even walked to the top of the viewing platform yet.

An escalator ride delivered us to a pedestal of the statue, which for perspective spanned the length of an RV. *Christ the Redeemer* itself rose to the height of a ten-story building, gleaming in the haze of spotlights that were still powered on. The night before, I was having dinner on Sugarloaf Mountain and had to step outside for a call. I remember looking across the water and seeing Corcovado Mountain in the distance. Clouds were swirling at its peak, and as they moved, the statue of *Christ the Redeemer* began to peek through. It was breathtaking.

It's one thing to admire the massive monument from afar; it's another to stand right in front of it. Proximity brings intimacy. The closer you get, the more you notice. Like the fact that the statue is not just concrete but entirely layered with a mosaic of triangular-shaped soapstone. When the statue was constructed during the mid- to late 1920s, the women of Rio attached the six million tiles with their bare hands.[1]

Facing the rising sun, the outstretched ninety-two-foot arms of *Christ the Redeemer* overlook Guanabara Bay and Sugarloaf Mountain. To the west of it, a lush rainforest. To the north, a cityscape of Rio rises with luxury high-rise apartments shaping the skyline of wealthy neighborhoods like Copacabana. As the sun hastened over the horizon, the beaches of Ipanema unveiled. Beyond it lay the expanse of the Atlantic Ocean. With our group being only a few in number, every step and whisper was amplified. I couldn't help but feel we were disturbing holy silence.

Each of us had time alone to soak in the shifting kaleidoscope of colors in the sky and the landscape coming to life below. Some marveled at the clouds that hovered close, soft and light as a trampoline. Others read the Bible or prayed. When the sun finally appeared in full crowning glory, I shared a message with the team.

It was hard to reconcile the sweeping vista with something I had read, seemingly echoed by some people in Rio: "Even Jesus turns His back on the poor."[2] This statement may crush the tenderhearted among us, but a glimpse into the area's history and a walk behind the statue reveal why those words were spoken. There you'll find beautiful greenery. Twenty-five-plus miles out in Duque de Caxias, a northern suburb of Rio de Janeiro, a restoration project is underway to bring back the natural mangrove landscape. You'd never believe what it looked like before 2012.

For thirty-four years, this region was home to Latin America's largest landfill, Jardim Gramacho.[3] About nine thousand tons of garbage—yogurt containers, used sanitary products, diapers, and rotting meat—were collected each day from some of the country's most affluent neighborhoods. It wasn't unusual to see dead bodies buried in the trash.[4] One time a dead baby was even found.[5] Toxic waste from the site oozed into Guanabara Bay, rendering the water unswimmable and devastating the local fishing community.[6]

The size of 243 football fields (yes, that's how I do math), this mountain of trash once represented job security to almost two thousand garbage pickers, *catadores* in Portuguese. The job title speaks for itself. Before the dump closed for good in 2012, these men, women, and even children would sift through a mountain of garbage, gathering recyclables like glass, scrap metal, and paper that they could either sell or turn into something useful like furniture and jewelry. The *catadores* kept some of the garbage for themselves, such as nearly empty shampoo bottles they could squeeze a few washes from and dirty toothbrushes they could boil the gunk out of. With a flashlight strapped under their chins and a headlamp, many hunted for trash at night to avoid the broiling sun.[7]

Whether at night, during the day, or sometimes both, *catadores* made a living wading through contaminated mud and muck. Inhaling methane gas from the rotting waste, they'd stuff barrels or bags to the brim with their treasures from trash. *Catadores* were not exclusive to Jardim Gramacho. Nor did the job vanish because the landfill was closed down. There are estimates of up to thirty thousand garbage pickers in the Rio area.[8] Throughout the country, *catadores* number almost a million.[9]

In a well-known documentary, this garbage dump has been described as "the end of the line. It's where everything not-good goes ... including the people."[10] A *catadore* noted, "The dump is pure suffering."[11] Another is quoted as saying, "In the garbage, there is no future."[12]

When people in that part of the world claim Jesus has turned His back on the poor, it appears that way due to the position of *Christ the Redeemer*. Based on its geography, the statue's open arms seem to invite a more desirable and affluent part of the region. I mean absolutely zero disrespect to the creator of this breathtaking monument when I say the feeling that Christ is showing favoritism to the rich, capable, or successful is not an accurate image of the gospel.

God's arms, and His heart, are open not only to the haves, to glistening fabled beaches, to parts of the world that flash green and gold. Nor do His arms reach out only to those who go to church every Sunday, haven't said a cuss word in the last sixty days, or volunteer at a nursing home once a month. His back is not turned toward anyone, at any time, at any place. The arms of Jesus extend to all.

The beauty of the gospel lies in its inclusivity. But Christ did more than display inclusivity through outstretched arms. He gave His life for all—*all*, not just some. In the beginning of this chapter, I introduced a word that altered the landscape of history: *sin*. The only way to really understand the gravity of redemption is to examine the reality of what caused cosmic chaos.

SIN, THE UNIVERSAL PROBLEM

Sin is the kind of word that makes some people cringe, squirm in their seats, or even roll their eyes. However uncomfortable the idea to some people, *sin*, which means "missing the mark for God's standard for humanity"[13] is a problem. It's evident in my life. I often miss the mark.

Sin is universal. We're born into it. We're all guilty of it. We've all felt its sting. I know I have. The reality of a broken world and a broken people is that without acceptance of God's intervention, we're stuck in

> The reality of a broken world and a broken people is that without acceptance of God's intervention, we're stuck in a cycle of spiritual and moral corruption.

a cycle of spiritual and moral corruption. Sin isn't just about breaking a rule or doing bad things—it's about breaking the relationship with the One who made us. Sin makes us guilty because it's a rejection of God's perfect standard of love, justice, and goodness. It's not just about personal preference or cultural norms; it points to something much bigger—objective morality. The very fact that we can call something wrong or evil points to a standard of what's truly right, and that standard comes from God Himself.

Adam and Eve's decision to disobey God by eating a piece of forbidden fruit had a far-reaching effect (Genesis 3). The universe's first couple didn't welcome sin into just their own lives—they brought it into the world. Paul said, "Therefore, just as sin entered the world through one man, and death through sin, . . . in this way death came to all people, because all sinned" (Romans 5:12).

When Adam and Eve sinned, our relationship with God was forever changed. Not only was our intimate connection with Him fractured, but disease, decay, and death were unleashed on every living thing. It's impossible to be human and not feel the effects of sin. This three-letter word means so much more than a list of things to avoid. It corrupts the royal essence of who we are and enslaves us to the will and whims of our broken nature. It leads to addiction, whether food, the bottle, sex, or the Place Order button. We become enslaved by what we think will satisfy us. Sin leads to greed, to taking what was never ours anyway and demanding our preferences be met. Sin is the reason we crave what may eventually hurt us and why we settle for quick fixes instead of permanent answers. Sin is both the pride and pain of man.

Whether we realize it or not, deep in our hearts we see what's broken in the world and long for wrong to be made right. How is it possible that at this very moment 1 out of every 150 people around the world is trapped in trafficking, stripped of their freedom, and robbed of their worth?[14] We inherently know something is very wrong with this picture.

Something deep within us recognizes injustice in many places. We know that no child, like Frantzky, should be denied medical care because of his or her appearance. Nor should any child or adult be exploited by those in power or systems put in place that are broken from the start.

A few years ago, gangs overtook a Caribbean village, destroying it and abandoning more than fifty children with special needs in a local orphanage. After the kids were rescued, someone discovered a young boy with severe special needs tied to a tree. Anyone could see that what was done to this boy is deplorable. But the image of God is defiled all the time, in places most of us will never travel to as well as neighborhoods right outside our front doors. Hearing stories like these pulls into focus the gravity of sin, from the actions it drives to the suffering it causes.

Sin lies at the root of our image problem. It's what drove a dark web offender to abuse children, teach others how to do the same, and evade capture for ten years. Hunted by prolific law enforcement agencies, a Florida man was finally arrested and found guilty of multiple charges related to child sexual abuse material (CSAM), including possession, production, and distribution of pornographic images as well as hands-on offenses. Authorities found in his possession 85,000 images of child sexual abuse material, 845 videos of child sexual abuse material, and 8,500 AI-generated

> Sin lies at the root of our image problem.

images of child sexual abuses.[15] Agents also found eleven pairs of children's underwear and five spy cameras in a locked drawer in his house.[16]

The consequence of sin? A depravity that doesn't end with harming the person involved but also pulls innocent victims into its grips.

Studies tell us that one out of three girls and one out of six boys will endure sexual abuse before they turn eighteen.[17] Next time you're in a restaurant or the mall, look around. You're likely walking past someone whose self-image is fractured and masked under a fake smile, a hoodie, or makeup.

Our souls cry out for restorative justice for a reason. The world needs it. The community longs for it. We do too.

Like a cancer that spreads when abnormal cells grow out of control, invading tissues and weakening the body's systems, sin spreads its roots far and wide. Sin, in any form, dehumanizes and diminishes. These consequences are not isolated to heinous crimes but saturate everyday life.

Think of the strife caused in marriages and families from jealousy or selfishness. Or how our words of gossip can cut deep. Or how dishonesty eats away, bite by bite, at authentic relationships. We all feel or bear scars from sin.

The brokenness that's attached to sin is personal. The struggle you have connecting with others? The emptiness you still feel after you get the raise, the relationship, or the role? The hunger for something more fulfilling than a creative outlet or a cool car? The inner turmoil that resists pills or pleasure? Whether a whisper or a shout, we ache for more than treasures that fade, love that comes with expiration dates, and days absent of purpose.

All our deepest longings—for significance, restorative order, sense out of chaos, deep and meaningful love—point to one Person.

WHAT ABOUT OUR ROYAL IMAGE?

Circling back to the question in the last chapter about the role of sin: Does it affect the status of our royal worth? I believe the short answer is no. I mentioned Genesis 5:1–3 in the last chapter, when God's image gets passed from Adam to his son Seth. Another image verse occurs a few chapters later in Genesis 9:6. It's interesting that these passages were written after sin had already wreaked havoc on the world. Two out of three image passages occur post-fall. It seems clear that our image, our value to God, remains intact, despite our failures. It's not earned. It can't be lost. While sin has broken us, it didn't damage or remove our royal worth.

As Dr. Imes wrote, "Identity is a modern concept, but a useful one for talking about the image of God. We can no more lose our identity as God's image than a child can lose his or her identity as a son or a daughter."[18] Not even sin and the death and destruction it brings can remove our worth to God. Since our worth does not have to do with our capacities or abilities, it stays the same. Dr. Imes continued, "Our relationship with God may be strained or broken, but humans remain the image of God."[19]

Still, we're broken. But there is hope.

Here's the thing about our human identity—the moment we realize we're not living up to who God created us to be is the moment we can start stepping into who we can be, made right and reconciled to His family.

I love the story of how *Christ the Redeemer* came to be. The initial idea had nothing to do with Jesus. Let's start with some context. Princess Isabel, the daughter of Emperor Pedro II, who ruled Brazil in the nineteenth century, was next in line for the throne after the infant deaths of both her brothers. Her eventual succession wasn't met with enthusiasm. For starters, she was a woman. She also had a strong faith and married a foreign prince.[20] These three strikes culminated in a military coup that ultimately toppled the monarchy, forcing Princess Isabel into exile in France. Before the fall of her family, however, she had used her power to do good.

Princess Isabel had acted as regent on three occasions while her father traveled abroad. In 1888, during her third regency, she signed the "Golden Law," officially abolishing slavery in Brazil—the last country in the Western world to do so.[21] In eighteen words, this legislation set free millions of slaves and shut down slave plantations for good.[22] The same year a proposal emerged to construct a statue in her honor.[23] The princess, who was hailed as a redemptress, respectfully declined. She had a better idea. Princess Isabel proposed a more fitting monument: a statue of Jesus, whom she called the true redeemer of mankind.[24] The idea wasn't revisited until the 1920s, when it finally led to the construction of this new wonder of the world.

Princess Isabel's choice to forgo a statue of herself in favor of one of Jesus says something far greater than her lack of desire for human recognition. The *Christ the Redeemer* statue stands as a symbol of the central truth of the gospel—God sent His Son, Jesus Christ, on a rescue mission for humanity. More specifically, to save us from what we couldn't save ourselves from, to restore our relationship with Him.

Perhaps you could call it the royal rescue.

Chapter 6

THE ROYAL RESCUE

THERE'S A STORY TOLD OF A YOUNG WOMAN WHO was caught speeding and brought before a judge. The judge read the charges against her and asked if she was guilty or not. "Guilty," the woman admitted. After slamming the gavel down to punctuate the verdict, he sentenced her to pay a fine. And then, in a moment that shocked the courtroom, the judge stood up from behind his bench, removed his robe, stepped down, and paid the fine with his own money.[1]

Why would a judge do this? Turns out, the judge was the guilty woman's father.

He both loved her and was required to uphold the law and enforce justice. He loved his daughter so much, in fact, that he was willing to take off his judicial robe, embrace his role as a dad, and pay her fine.[2]

What a beautiful picture. God is a holy God, a just judge, and a loving father. Justice exacts a price for wrongdoing, and Love finds a way to satisfy that penalty. Paul put it like this: "God made him who had no sin to be sin for us, so that in him we might become the righteousness of God" (2 Corinthians 5:21).

As I've heard it said, God treated Jesus as if He had committed our sins, so He could treat us as if we had lived Jesus' perfect life. Thirty-plus years after giving my life to Jesus, I still get goosebumps when I think of the earth-shattering reality that He took on my sin so that I can be forgiven and live with Him forever. Even though sin made me guilty, God provided a way out. And as a result, my royal image—and yours and everyone else's—can now be in right standing with the Father.

What a God!

LOVE COMES DOWN

In a moment that seems ordinary, the greatest love story unfolds. Before Jesus grew from the size of a bean to a full-fledged baby in Mary's belly, before His first newborn cry shattered a holy hush, before He nestled and nursed in His mother's arms, the biblical narrative prepares us for the unfolding drama.

Throughout Scripture, beginning in the Old Testament, Jesus is reflected in prophetic and—get this!—kingdom language. Let's look at this thread together.

If Genesis 1–2 highlights the value of humankind, then Genesis 3 can be seen as the downfall of humankind. Thank God we're not parked in that place of hopelessness. There was (and is) good news! To the crafty serpent who feeds off the chaos it created, God promised, "I will put enmity between you and the woman, and between your offspring and hers; he will crush your head, and you will strike his heel" (Genesis 3:15). Just three chapters into the biblical story, Jesus and redemption are already in view.

This verse whispers hope into the devastation of the fall. The serpent's apparent triumph to corrupt God's image was overshadowed by a promise: A descendant of Eve would rise to crush the power of evil once and for all. The royal rescue had been initiated.

As the narrative continues, glimpses of this coming Savior appear all throughout the Old Testament. In the ark that saved Noah and his family from judgment, we see a picture of Jesus, the true Ark, who shields us from the wrath of sin. In the ram provided for Abraham on Mount Moriah, we see a foreshadowing of the Lamb of God who takes away the sin of the world (John 1:29). In the covenant with David, a King was promised whose throne would endure forever (2 Samuel 7). In the Psalms, a Messiah is envisioned who sits at God's right hand, ruling as both King and Priest (Psalm 110). In the prophecies of Isaiah, the birth of a child is predicted whose name would be "Wonderful Counselor, Mighty God, Everlasting Father, Prince of Peace" (Isaiah 9:6-7). As you can see, Jesus is reflected through prophetic and kingdom language.

By the time we reach the New Testament, the royal thread becomes a golden cord. From the genealogy of Adam to the law of Moses, the story of Scripture comes to a crescendo in the moment when the Word would become flesh and dwell among us (John 1:14). This was the plan all along. Jesus came down from heaven and assumed an earthly position. God took on human flesh. The Author of life entered our story. Matthew opened his Gospel by identifying Jesus as the "son of David" (Matthew 1:1), tying Him directly to the Davidic covenant. Even the Greek word for "gospel" (*euangelion*) carried royal connotations in ancient Greco-Roman literature; it was used to announce the birth or victory of a king.[3] The declaration of the gospel, then, was not merely good news but royal news: The true King had come.

Every covenant, every promise, every prophecy was a detail in God's rescue plan. Jesus Himself announced this royal mission when

He said, "The time has come . . . The kingdom of God has come near. Repent and believe the good news!" (Mark 1:15).

It's no coincidence that the birth of our Savior was announced to shepherds. In the first century in that part of the world, shepherds were poor and not esteemed. On society's ladder, they were set on a very low rung.[4] And yet, these less-than outcasts were the first to receive the announcement of Jesus' birth. Love truly does come down to all.

In this one scene, the world is turned upside down. And this was just the beginning. During His thirty-three years on earth, Jesus introduced a whole new way of living. His teaching, transformative by cultural and religious standards, offered an alternative lens to see, treat, and value people. Unlike the powers of His time, Jesus promised a kingdom of true freedom—a life liberated from death, the inevitable wage of sin. All it cost was His life. And in a willing act, Jesus was crucified on a cross. The priceless blood of our Savior was spilled and the weight of sin—my sin and yours—was upon Him.

Jesus experienced even more than a physical death; He endured a spiritual demise of being separated from His Father. Jesus was forsaken so we don't have to be. Jesus was abandoned so we don't have to be. The Father turned His back on Jesus, His Son, so He wouldn't have to turn His back on us.

Jesus didn't just die on the cross; He gave up His life. No one took it from Him. He said, "No one takes it from me, but I lay it down of my own accord" (John 10:18). The cross wasn't forced on Jesus—He chose it. And that makes all the difference. His sacrifice wasn't just about suffering; it was about willingly stepping into our place, taking on our sin, and restoring what had been broken.

Three days after He was buried, Jesus defeated death. And with that same power, He offers us eternal life. C. S. Lewis wrote that Jesus "has forced open a door that has been locked since the death of the first man. He has met, fought, and beaten the King of Death. Everything is different because He has done so. This is the beginning of the New Creation: a new chapter in cosmic history has opened."[5]

Jesus didn't just show up one night as a surprise twist. The biblical narrative reveals that the Son of God was present from the very beginning. From the garden to the manger to the cross and beyond, Scripture tells a royal love story. A King steps down from His throne, wraps Himself in humanity, and conquers through sacrificial love. The Son of David is the Son of God, and His kingdom is unshakable. The thread of royalty, woven through every book of the Bible, ties together the greatest love story ever told: the love of a King who came down to bring His people home.

> From the garden to the manger to the cross and beyond, Scripture tells a royal love story.

Whether we look forward from creation or backward from the cross, royalty and redemption is always in view. Jesus, the ultimate image of God in flesh, stands in the center of it all. As Dr. Imes put it,

> For Jesus to become human meant that He became the image of God—a physical representative of God's presence whose most important task is to glorify the Creator. The New Testament calls Jesus "the image of the invisible God" because he is like every other human (Colossians 1:15). However, Jesus is not like every other human because he lives in complete alignment with the will of God. Unlike us, Jesus is fully surrendered to the Father, fully committed to living out his vocation as God's image. He's able "to reconcile to himself all things . . . by making peace through his blood, shed on the cross" (Colossians 1:20). Through his self-giving love, Jesus opens a path for us to encounter the one whose image we are.[6]

Jesus didn't give His life as a sacrifice without purpose. He was born, lived, died, and rose again to bring you and me back to the Father. This was a rescue mission, the greatest one in the world.

BEYOND FORGIVENESS

There have been times in my life when forgiving someone has felt much like digging through stone with a plastic spoon. Ever been there? It's not easy to forgive someone who has done us wrong. Our natural tendency is to hold tightly to grudges. But for Jesus, the opposite is true. He willingly gave up His last breath so we could be forgiven. And He doesn't hold it against us. He's not blowing up our phones to constantly remind us of our guilt. My sin—my failures, my stubbornness, and my many self-centered decisions—may have nailed Jesus to the cross, but He never throws it in my face. Can you believe how good God is?

The life, death, and resurrection of Jesus assures us of forgiveness, eternal life, and adoption as God's children. But there's a piece that often gets overlooked. While sin forgiveness usually gets the limelight—and should—we must not forget the equally profound reality of reconciliation.

When we talk about salvation, we emphasize Jesus' sacrifice and the forgiveness of our sin, and we should. But if we stop there, we're telling only part of the story. God's goal wasn't just to bring us from spiritual debt to a zero balance. It wasn't just about getting us back to neutral. His aim is far greater—full reconciliation, a restored relationship, and being made righteous in His sight. Imagine having someone pay off your debt and taking it one step further by filling your bank account with limitless funds. That's what Jesus came to do for us. Not only did He erase the sin that separated us from God, He also made us sons and daughters and invited us to be a part of His royal family. We get to come close to God. He wants us to!

The word used in the New Testament for reconciliation means the restoration of relationship. The Greek word *katallasso* was an old monetary term for exchanging coins.[7] It was also commonly used to change "someone from an enemy into a friend."[8] To reconcile is to reestablish a proper relationship after it has been broken. Think of reconciliation as a means to

> be one again,
> make things right,
> take away separation, and
> bring peace between parties.

The story of the prodigal son in the Bible paints one of the best pictures of the essence of reconciliation.

A SON COMES HOME

Luke 15 records what to many Christians is the familiar story of a father and his two sons. I'm guessing here, but from what I read, the oldest son had the typical traits of firstborns. Eager to please, he took his responsibilities seriously. The youngest was more of a rebel. He pressured his father for an early inheritance and, wasting no time, left home to indulge in a life of partying. And as some of us know, one day, exhausted from the outcome of his self-destructive ways, the youngest son decided it was time to come home. Chewed up by worry, the son wasn't sure how his dad would react. This is what the Bible says about the homecoming:

> So he got up and went to his father. But while he was still a long way off, his father saw him and was filled with compassion for him; he ran to his son, threw his arms around him and kissed him. (Luke 15:20)

Let's start with the father. If you picture the scene in your mind, the elder wasn't watering the garden or getting the mail and just happened to see his youngest son walking toward him. It wasn't a coincidence. The father never stopped looking for his son. He didn't have to look again. His eyes were on the horizon since the day the young man took off. For those of you who may be far from our Father in heaven, know He's looking for you. And He has never taken His eyes off you.

When the Bible tells us the dad "ran to his son," those words carry a deeper truth than what appears on the surface. In Middle Eastern culture, it was considered undignified for a man to run. Wearing long tunics, not modern-day joggers and tees, they would have to lift their robes to avoid tripping. This act revealed their legs—not a turnoff, but a cultural taboo of indecent exposure.[9] So why would the father run?

In ancient tight-knit communities, a Jewish son who lost his inheritance would endure public shaming. In a ceremony called the *kezazah*, the Homeowner's Association of that day would shatter a large pot at the boy's feet, hurling insults and declaring him cast out from the neighborhood. According to several scholars, the father may have raced toward his son not only out of heartfelt joy but most likely to shield the boy from prying eyes witnessing the disgrace.[10] Whether to protect his son from being stoned or shamed, the father ran so he could pay the price.

What a powerful scene! In a response filled with compassion, the father endured shame to keep it from landing where it should have been thrown—on his son. The Greek word used for "compassion" is *splagchnizomai* (pronounced *splunk'-knee-so-my*). This word reflects a deep-seated emotion—to be moved in the inner parts, the bowels, the seat of fierce passions like love.[11]

The story of the prodigal son is more than a heartwarming reunion between a father and his offspring. It reflects God's heart for every human being. Because the Father sent His only Son, Jesus, to endure life, death, and resurrection, we can be made right with God. And equally as wonderful, we are invited to be part of His family.

Our royal blood as God's image never stopped flowing through our human veins, but, just like in the parable of the prodigal, sin created relational separation. We are not able to come home on our own. We needed the Father to do what we couldn't do. We needed Jesus to restore our original intimacy with God.

THE BOY AND THE CARDBOARD BOX

I was born and spent the first few years of my life in the Philippines. My dad often tells me about the time when we were living there and he had to travel to Manila, the capital, to meet his team.

I may be biased, but in my opinion the Philippines is known for some of the nicest people in the world. It's also known for its chaotic traffic. From personal experience, it's not unusual to spend a few hours driving fifteen miles.

Picture five official lanes of one-way traffic looking more like eight. Motorcycles carve their own paths and weave through gaps so tight it looks like at any second one of them is going to slam into a car. At the same time, street vendors dart between the stalled traffic, shouting for your attention to purchase their wares, snacks, and phone chargers. Horns blare in not-so-harmonious symphony without tangible results. I mean, you're still stuck in the same place for thirty minutes to an hour. As your head pounds in rhythmic fury, a peddler shoves a bouquet through your open window, just one more thing, you're told, that you cannot live without.

Dad sits in traffic when he spots a little boy wearing just a T-shirt lying beside a cardboard box on a median. Covered in soot and dirt, with frayed edges and sagging corners, the box has seen better days. Dad asks the other passengers in the car if they know who the boy is. No one does. My father feels a tug on his heart. God whispers, *This boy is your son.*

Accompanied by one of the local pastors in his car, Dad walks over to the sleeping boy and gently taps his shoulder. The boy looks to be five or six years old. Jutting ribs cling to transparent skin. His gaunt face is dusted with exhaust smoke. Startled by the presence of my father, the boy curls his dirt-covered fingers over his bony knees and hugs them close to his chest.

"You don't know me," Dad says softly, his voice gentle. "We've just met, but I want you to know that I'd love for you to be part of our family. I promise to give you my best, to treat you like my own son, and to love you. Would you like that? Would you like to be part of my family?"

The boy's eyes grow wide as his hands tremble. Suddenly, he shoots up from the cardboard floor. With one hand he grabs the few trinkets littered around him. With the other, he snatches the box in his tiny fingers. Then, the skeletal figure darts off, vanishing into the cacophony of street chaos. My dad's stomach drops. He begins to weep. My mom still talks about how that moment crushed my dad for months.

When reflecting on this incident later, my dad shared that just like that boy ran away from him, we often run from God's personal invitation to accept a new life in Him. Rather than receive the greatest gift, we look the other way, clinging instead to our trinkets—our platform, preferences, possessions, passions, pride, and plans. God longs to give us His very best! What does that mean exactly? He invites us to come home. He desires deep relationship. He wants us to become a new creation. He wants to give us purpose.

> God longs to give us His very best!

I wonder if today you're running or thinking about running from God. If so, it's time to stop. It's time to come home. It's time to say yes to His invitation to forgive and reconcile you back to His family.

Maybe today is the day you say yes to Jesus. It's a big decision, but it's a simple one. Jesus has already said yes to you, offering the free gift of eternal life. He loves you deeply—so much that He knows every detail about your life, the highs and the lows. He cares about you and wants to have a personal relationship with you. If you've never accepted Jesus, now could be the time.

If you've been hurt by a church or its leaders and feel distant from God because of it, I invite you to set aside the pain for a moment and look again. If you're ready, I'd love to lead you in a prayer. It's not about magic words but about your heart saying yes to the One who loves you. Here's the prayer:

Dear Jesus,

I believe that You died on the cross for me. I put my faith in You and ask You to come into my heart. Forgive me for everything I've done wrong. Thank You for loving me and making me Your masterpiece. I want to live for You.
In Jesus' name, amen.

If you just prayed that prayer for the first time, God has a smile on His face. He's never stopped looking at you. Welcome to your new family in Christ. Know that God is with you, always, and He has a plan for your life.

John 3:16 reminds us that God doesn't turn His back on anyone—"For God so loved the *world* that he gave his one and only Son, that whoever believes in him shall not perish but have eternal life." Out of everything in all creation, the only thing Jesus chose to die for was people. That's how valuable you and I are to Him.

THE ULTIMATE PRICE

In our society we typically decide the worth of an item by how much we are willing to pay for it. But that's an entirely inaccurate formula. Something that costs one hundred dollars today may cost seventy-five next week. That expensive tech gadget you bought yesterday? Power it on and it immediately decreases in worth. Value increases and plummets.

Whether we connect our worth to academic success, our contributions to society, attractiveness, or how long we pray, when we base our self-worth on external factors, we might as well hop on a roller coaster and buckle up. We might feel a rush of adrenaline, but relying on it can mask or erode our true identity. Our self-worth should be based on something greater like our God-given identity. Unlike a new car that immediately depreciates when it's driven off a lot, this worth never fades.

Whether you've been a Christian for years or just made the decision to trust in Jesus, spend a few minutes thinking about what defines your worth as a human being.

Is it work? Is your value measured by your performance at the office, on the field, in the boardroom?

Is it the approval of others? Is your worth measured by being accepted, appreciated, and validated?

Is it influenced by what you look like?

Does it have anything to do with how much money you make or how many likes you've gotten on your last social media post?

Now think about the worth you attach to others. Do you value other people by any of the above measurements? Do you see other people through the lens of what they wear, what language they speak, or what they can do for you?

Before you continue reading, spend some time thinking about your value.

Read the next statement slowly: If you're searching for a true reflection of your worth, look no further than the cross. You are worth Jesus' life, His death, and His resurrection. That's how much He paid to invite you back home. There's no better image to illustrate how God's love redefined your value, and mine, forever. Ask yourself, *What would change if I saw myself how God sees me?*

> If you're searching for a true reflection of your worth, look no further than the cross. You are worth Jesus' life, His death, and His resurrection.

Chapter 7

WHAT OUR ROYAL STATUS MEANS

LILY WAS BORN IN HAITI ON APRIL 28, 2012, TWO years after the country's devastating earthquake. Born with arthrogryposis, a congenital condition that restricts leg movements and causes severe deformity, she faced significant medical challenges from the start. On May 10, Lily's mother surrendered her to a local orphanage, noting her need for more medical care.

Meanwhile, about a year earlier, in Birmingham, Alabama, Jennifer Dobson and her family felt called to welcome a child into their home through adoption. They set the wheels in motion, and by the time Lily was born, Jennifer had already been praying for her as well as her birth parents, even though Jennifer didn't yet know who they were. When the opportunity to be matched with Lily came to fruition, the Dobsons hesitated. Convinced that caring for a child with complex medical needs was too hard, they doubted Lily was the right match. After much prayer and reflection, however, God assured them that Lily was the perfect fit for their family.

Over three and a half years, the Dobsons made six trips to Haiti, navigating stalled paperwork, a resistant adoption agency, and constantly shifting legal requirements. Heartbreaking delays ensued as Lily's parents struggled with failed attempts to secure a medical visa, essential for her urgent health-care needs. When the Dobsons finally obtained a short-term medical visa, they were forced to renew it repeatedly over two years to address Lily's worsening health while pursuing her adoption in the United States.

During this time, Lily endured about thirteen intense surgeries. During one surgery, doctors installed fixators in her legs, requiring daily adjustments to correct her bones. The Dobsons faced one final, intense hurdle when immigration nearly deported Lily due to missing documentation from Haiti. When Lily was five, the Dobsons were finally able to adopt her. Two years later, she became a US citizen. This marked the end of a nearly seven-year journey filled with immense physical, legal, and emotional challenges. For the Dobsons, it also ushered in a new life together, filled with its own set of pits and peaks.

Jennifer remembers one of the first times she was on a plane with Lily during the adoption process. Staring at her daughter's thick eyelashes, Jennifer wrote:

> I finally realized what God's love for me really felt like. I love this child so deeply who isn't my blood, who did not grow in my belly, who is not the same color as me . . . I realized how much my Father in Heaven loves me and what adoption into His family really feels like. It was the first time I felt Him looking at me, the way I was looking at her . . . and it was overwhelming. For God *so loved* me that He gave me Jesus. That He made a way for me. That He continually fought for me and did not give up on me when it seemed hopeless. It was the first time I saw and felt with clear eyes the magnitude of His love for me, and in that moment I could not have felt

more like a child cradled in her Father's arms than Lily did in mine. I am forever grateful to Him for how Lily's story has continued. I am forever grateful to Him for continuing to make a way. I am forever grateful to Him for bringing her home, because He brought her home. I am most grateful for His continued love to take me deeper and show me more of whom He is.[1]

Through adopting Lily, Jennifer caught a glimpse into the love God has for her—and for all humankind. It's a love that surpasses every obstacle, disability, doubt, and barrier. This love, revealed through our royal identity and the invitation to be reconciled to God through the life, death, and resurrection of Jesus, is transforming. When we see who we truly are in God, we can't help but be changed.

If you're having trouble grasping the royal reality stamped on your life, I want to offer you three truths to help reveal what this means to you in real, practical ways.

- We are created to be—not bear—God's image.
- You are one of one.
- We are made to represent God.

My prayer is that you'll ask God to help unlock these truths in your life.

WE ARE CREATED TO BE— NOT BEAR—GOD'S IMAGE

In one of my conversations with Dr. Imes, she said something I jotted down and began to process over time. She wrote this same statement in her book: "God's image is not something we bear; it's something we are... 'image' is not something we do, but who we are."[2]

Wait, what?

If you're a Christian, you've probably heard it said that we are image bearers of God. *Shoot*, that statement is one of our nonnegotiables at the foundation. Being raised in the church all my life, that's how I'd understood it. But the deeper I dug, the more I began to understand Imes's point.

The meaning of the phrase "to bear" is "to hold up; support or to hold or remain firm under (a load)."[3] In a physical sense, we might swing a heavy bag over our shoulder or roll a bowling ball down the center of an oil-coated lane. We can also bear choices—we decide to pursue or leave a particular career, take up a new hobby like pickleball, or change perspectives dependent on newfound knowledge.

But who we are is, well, who we are.

Our status as being created in God's image is static. It's not a label, uniform, sign, or mask we pick up one moment and drop the next. It's intrinsic. It makes us human. Imes said it like this: "Because the essence of being God's image is a claim about our identity rather than a capability or function, we cannot lose it."[4] If you're a parent and your child rebels and walks away from relationship with you, there may be separation, but your son or daughter is no less your child. He or she is still your son or daughter. Similarly, we cannot lose our status as God's image, despite our sin, addictions, or even disbelief.

I find it meaningful to say that, rather than bearing His image, we are created to *be* His image. We are God's image *beings*, not image *bear*ers. For those of you who have always identified humans as image bearers, this new language might take some getting used to. Let's dig deeper.

The state of *being* typically gets overshadowed by *doing* or another measurement used to determine our worth, such as where we went to school, who we know, or our country of origin. Consider how this can play out in Christian circles. Does your perceived worth seem to tick up when your numbers at your Bible study increase or if your quiet time stretches past thirty minutes?

> We are God's image *beings*, not image *bear*ers.

Who we are, as God's image, is foundational. It comes first. Everything else bounces off that launching pad, including whatever *doing* we were born to do. Our identity is not our doing; it informs our doing.

Being is at the core of who God is, so it's only natural that being comes first. Before Moses informed God of his perceived disability, Moses asked God a question about his identity. "Suppose I go to the Israelites and say to them, 'The God of your fathers has sent me to you,' and they ask me, 'What is his name?' Then what shall I tell them?" (Exodus 3:13). When God is asked His name, He doesn't introduce Himself as the Master of the Universe who formed and filled for six days or as the Great Astronomer who hung every star in the sky or as the Great Biologist who crafted humanity out of dust. I mean, He could have. These details were obviously true and certainly would have gained Him, and Moses as His rep, instant cred.

God's response, however, helps inform the meaning of identity—"I AM WHO I AM. This is what you are to say to the Israelites: 'I AM has sent me to you'" (Exodus 3:14).

I AM.

Two words literally sum up everything about God. He is self-sufficient and self-sustaining. He is the God who was, who is, and who will be.[5]

Guess who else used this same moniker? In one of many instances when the religious leaders in His time challenged His authority, Jesus clapped back at their questions with a simple but loaded statement: "Very truly I tell you . . . before Abraham was born, I am!" (John 8:58).

I AM.

When we introduce ourselves to people, many of us tend to lead with our given names, our vocation, our passions—whatever we imagine in that moment will connect the person before us to who we are. But God doesn't see us through those things. Being His image underscores first and foremost our identity. Our doing pours from identity. It's not the other way around. As an image *being* of God, our worth isn't tied to achievements, jobs, social status, or athletic ability. It's not about what we've done, haven't done, or wish we could do. Our worth is derived from who we are as God's creation. We are His masterpiece.

Look in the mirror. Look past the color of your eyes, your rosy cheeks, your matted locks, your ringlets, your glass skin, or the acne that's never gone away. Look beyond the name you hate or the one you love. Look beyond the failed presentation or the trophy you just got awarded. Look beyond the opinions that crushed your confidence or filled you with pride. No matter what others say or how harshly your inner critic judges you, there's a core worth in you that nothing (and no one) can take away.

I wish I'd known this truth sooner. It would have spared me so much stress and anxiety over feeling I'd messed everything up. Knowing that God still sees His image in me, even through my mistakes and moments of anger, humbles and encourages me. And it moves me to do the same for others.

I've been fortunate to work with pastors and chaplains involved in prison ministry, speaking in some of the toughest environments with inmates who are there because of serious offenses. Whenever I take a ministry team along with me, I make one thing clear: They must view the inmates through the lens of what Jesus has done for them rather than seeing them through the offenses that have put them behind bars.

This is what it means to be God's image. We don't size someone up because of something awful that's happened to them or something awful they did to someone else. We don't lessen anyone's worth because they've broken the law, have made a horrible mistake willfully, or were at the wrong place at the wrong time. We use our image *being* vision and see the worth and value God has given them.

This is not always easy. I don't know about you, but it can be really hard for me. Whenever I'm tempted to judge others through a humanistic lens, I try to remember my sin. I try to think about all the times I didn't do the right thing and just wasn't caught. I try to remind myself I'm part of the reason Jesus agreed to die and reconcile us back to the Father. I reflect on the truth that "there is no one righteous, not even one" (Romans 3:10). I don't let myself forget that I'm one of the chief sinners who nailed Jesus to the cross. And guess what? God still made me in His image. With that in mind, how can I not share His love and show others their worth?

If God sees infinite value and dignity in every single one of us, we need to start seeing that in ourselves. And when we do, the truth will flow out of us to the people around us.

> If God sees infinite value and dignity in every single one of us, we need to start seeing that in ourselves.

YOU ARE ONE OF ONE.

A friend of mine shared with me a story I've never forgotten. There was a point in his life he was stuck in a downward spiral, battling suicidal thoughts. His lack of self-worth pushed him to believe the lie that he was better off dead. During what was the lowest period of my friend's life, he had the opportunity to talk to a former president of the United States.

With genuine concern that reflected his generous and thoughtful nature, the president offered encouragement. The words that stuck with my friend had to do with beetles. Yes, that's right, beetles. Stay with me, I promise I'll come back to the point.

The bombardier beetle, aptly named the "dinner date from hell,"[6] has an interesting defense mechanism. When threatened, it releases a chemical blast of intense heat and pressure. This noxious bomb is squirted at about five hundred bursts in one second.[7] This defense is so effective that it works even after a bombardier beetle is swallowed by a predator. The beetle's spray forces the predator to spit it out.[8] I know, I'm getting nauseous myself. Former rocket scientist and spacecraft pioneer Dr. Henry Richter emphasized that all of this must happen perfectly, otherwise the beetle will blow itself up.[9]

This complex design in an insect smaller than a fingernail points to divine craftsmanship. It's pretty unique. Did you know there are more than five hundred species of bombardier beetles alone? What's even wilder is that there are more than four hundred thousand different species of beetles in general.[10] This variety is astounding!

Time to connect the dots. The president reminded my friend that if God would create four hundred thousand unique beetle species, how much more intentional is He with us? "Don't you think God intentionally made each of us a little different?" the former commander in chief asked my friend, reminding him of the uniqueness with which he was created. The same is true for you.

You are truly one of a kind. Better yet, you are one of one!

Out of 8.2 billion people on this planet, there is no one like you.[11] There's no one like me either. There's no one like your best friend, your mom, your baby nephew, the barista who makes your coffee, or the teenager you pass every day while taking your dog for a walk.

> You are truly one of a kind. Better yet, you are one of one!

While scientists may be able to clone a person's genes, there's a reason they have failed in cloning an individual—God created each one of us unique. You and I have different genetics and gene expression, as well as different environmental influences and life experiences that are distinct from each other and from anyone else on the planet. We are incapable of being someone other than ourselves. Identical twins are not even identical. Though their fingerprints are similar in pattern, they are not the same. Same with their DNA. While almost identical, there are an average of 5.2 mutations in DNA between identical twins.[12]

So, yes, you are absolutely one of one. Being different is not a curse or a trait to despise; it's an intentional divine design. God doesn't create duplicates. He doesn't look at the world and think, *I need six of the same person*. Think about the wonders of the world. They captivate us because they're each one of a kind. I've visited many of them over the years, and I love how each one is uniquely different. They may all be different, but each one is a wonder in its own way.

One of my friends has a daughter who has endured much bullying because she is a little person. I hugged her dad the other night and encouraged him, reminding him of a simple but powerful truth: God didn't accidentally make her shorter or different out of some passing whim. She's not a random outcome or a happenstance. Just like if she had been created at six foot three instead, she is loved intentionally, formed with a purpose in mind, just as she is.

You don't have to prove your uniqueness for that to be true. There is something God placed in you that sets you apart from *every* animal, *every* plant, *every* mountain, *every* other human being, and *every* creation under heaven. You carry something within you that is extraordinary and unique from your classmates, your parents, your spouse, and your crew. You are not just another face in the crowd; you are an *ambassador* of God's character. He chose *you* to showcase His love, His mercy, His truth, in a way no other creature can. God never had and never will have an "oops" moment. You are God's image *being*. You are one of one!

WE ARE MADE TO REPRESENT GOD

Digital watermarks are everywhere, from TikTok and stock photo logos to gaming captures, video editing apps, and branded content. They are used to ensure authenticity, ownership, and credit across platforms. You may not always see these invisible signatures, but they are there.

As humans, we carry a watermark of our own: God's image. Regardless of belief in God or faith in Jesus Christ, every person has this divine signature, reflecting our Creator and intrinsic value. Though sin distorts how clearly we reflect God's qualities—like kindness, patience, justice, and love—it doesn't erase our "watermark."

We were designed to represent God.

At the core of being human we represent something bigger than ourselves. We see this in the early Jesus movement. Christians were helping those who Greco-Roman society looked past. You even have an early critic of Christianity say that it was a religion of "slaves, women, and little children."[13] Although this was Celsus' attempt to mock and belittle Christianity, Christianity from the start emphasized the value and dignity of all people. We even see that historically over the last two thousand some years.

According to historian Tom Holland, Christianity has shaped the modern world we live in today.[14] From hospitals to universities to human rights.[15] Of course, Christians haven't always acted like saints. Plenty of damage has been done in the name of "God." But don't let the messenger diminish the message. Because the Bible promotes a different ethic—one of grace, love, and justice—the world has been flipped upside down. Christians didn't create some new ideology that forced them to love their neighbor. No, they just leaned on God's value statement in Genesis 1:26–27 and, because of Christ, have been empowered to represent God like originally instructed from the very beginning.

We were made to represent God. A zebra can't do that. A tree can't do that. Only we can.

Many times over the years, I've probably represented sports teams better than I've represented God. So now I'm determined—though I still fail at times—to wear His image with the same passion, if not more, than I've shown for other things. Knowing the truth about our royal identity has been a game changer for me. It's challenged me to think about how I treat people and what it means to be God's image.

Knowing the truth in principle is one thing, but putting it into practice is the real sweet spot. How many times have I overlooked or ignored someone stamped with God's image because I was caught up in my priorities? How many divine appointments have I walked past because I was too busy or too distracted to recognize the royalty in someone standing right in front of me? Too many to count! God's principles aren't just meant to be believed, they are meant to be practiced. And if I don't put them into practice, do I really believe them?

Learning the royal truth about the worth of every human being has challenged me to scrutinize how I treat my loved ones and total strangers. It's urged me to question whether my thoughts, words, and actions consistently affirm the dignity of every person. It's caused me to regularly ask myself how I can better live out the belief that every person reflects God's image, especially with those I might overlook or judge.

I'm still very much in the process of trying my best to practice honoring God's image in others. Despite failing at times, I strive every day to hold myself accountable to how I see and treat other people. No matter how wrong I think someone is, how frustrated or annoyed I am at them, how often they may drop from my radar or never get into my line of sight to begin with, no matter how little I think I have in common with them, I am called to see every person with dignity and worth—not as objects, tools for my own goals, or pawns in a larger plan but as royal reflections of God's image. With this understanding, I have a duty to use my platform and every resource entrusted to me as God's representative.

Guess what? You're in on this too! Being God's image comes with the responsibility of representation. I'll develop this idea further in the third part of this book, but for the moment it's key to understand that recognizing and accepting your royal worth has far-reaching effects. One way or another, it will show up in how you live and what you do.

NO LIMITS

I want to introduce you to Trenton Hill. If Trenton can believe that God can use him as His image, then my hope is that as you read his story, you'll look outward and see that no disability can limit the power of a life God has chosen to use.

At birth, Trenton was diagnosed with cerebral palsy, a congenital disorder that impairs a person's ability to move and maintain balance and posture. He's used a power wheelchair since he was in preschool.

While he could once stand and walk with a walker, his physical limitations have gradually increased. Now he relies on an aide for most daily tasks.

Since he was five, Trenton knew there was something different about him. He couldn't run around and play tag like the other kids, nor could he throw a baseball. He couldn't hold a Lego between his fingers, let alone build a pirate ship out of the tiny building bricks. He couldn't even brush his teeth, comb his hair, or pour and drink a glass of milk on his own. And at that young age, Trenton also knew that God had a purpose for him beyond his physical limitations.

He would constantly tell his mom, Liz, *"God put me here for a reason."* It became his defining motto. As the years passed and difficulties grew, that quiet assurance morphed into a calling. Trenton desired to become a pastor and share God's love around the world. To most of us, this vision would seem ill-fitting. How can a person who still spends many hours every week in and out of doctors' offices and physical therapy, takes five times as long as able-bodied people to go to the bathroom and maneuver in and out of a car, and struggles with slurred speech be a messenger for the gospel?

God put me here for a reason.

When I met Trenton in September 2023, the first thing I noticed about him was his fresh cut. I'd never seen such a sharp hairstyle. The top of his head was styled in a crew cut, while the rest was shaved clean except for three words that rose from his scalp in crew cut fashion starting just above his left ear.

It read: God Is Able. The words were more than a spiritual catchphrase. They carried great meaning.

Liz shared with me that although he is typically optimistic, there are times doubt surfaces and threatens his hope. Around the time I met him, Trenton started feeling like his God-given desire to be a pastor was out of reach. He began to question what felt like a pipe dream. Then, he heard a sermon by Steven Furtick on Gideon from Judges 6. In this story, God called Gideon to lead Israel against the Midianites. Like Moses, Gideon was shocked—surely God had picked the wrong guy. After all, he was the kind of person who saw himself as the one chosen last in gym class. But God called this apprehensive would-be commander a "mighty warrior" and told him to "go in the strength you have and save Israel out of Midian's hand" (Judges 6:14).

Something moved Trenton deep within. Then the worship band played their song "More Than Able." The lyrics highlight God's ability to do more than we can imagine, exceeding our expectations. That even when we see obstacles, God sees miracles waiting to happen. In that moment, everything clicked for Trenton. He was reminded of his own dream to "go" and share God's message. Doubt crept in—*But I'm disabled. What can I do?* As Trenton prayed and surrendered his doubts, a thought pierced through: *What happens when you place "Go" in front of "disable"?* The answer came: *God. Is. Able.*

> *What happens when you place "Go" in front of "disable"?* The answer came: *God. Is. Able.*

Trenton shared this revelation with his barber, Fly Ty, also a local radio host. Blown away, Fly Ty immediately reached out to Pastor Steven, who happened to be one of his regulars. That summer, Trenton's story rippled through messages Pastor Steven shared on his tour, touching lives far beyond anything Trenton could have imagined. When he met me a few weeks later, he got his haircut with those three words as a reminder that with God anything is possible. Thank you, Trenton. I need that reminder!

My friend's confidence isn't rooted in the things society glorifies—like an Ivy League degree, celebrity connections, or a show-stopping talent for storytelling. Instead, it comes from his royal identity. He knows it—and it shows.

Trenton worked as an intern for Elevation Church in the summer of 2024. As part of the program, he was required to give a seven-minute sermon in front of a room full of other interns and staff. Liz said he was so nervous. At one point, he had decided he couldn't go through with it. But faith prevailed and God's power overcame the weakness Trenton thought he brought to the table. Here's a snippet of what he said:

> We are not competent in ourselves, but our competence comes from God . . . I just love how God has used me in such powerful ways and reminds me again that even though I'm in this chair, God can still work. I feel I am already chosen, I'm already loved, and Jesus has all power and authority. I just wanted to encourage you guys today that no matter what you're going through, Jesus already has that covered. . . . God can move mountains. He can turn bones into armies. He can do everything because He's God and He has given you everything you need for the season that you're in. So whatever battle you're facing today, just know that God is able to use you, whether it's speaking or encouraging someone or just putting a smile on someone's face. You may not be on the stage, but guess what? You're on a stage in Him![16]

Trenton's dream to be a pastor and share the message of God's love? Already happening! I know this first sermon is one of many to come. This is only the beginning for Trenton.

For much of my life, I've had the opportunity to experience incredible things—whether winning trophies, visiting the most beautiful parts of the world, meeting presidents, or speaking to a viewing crowd of millions. The most impactful opportunity might surprise you.

What has both wrecked and fueled my heart most deeply has been meeting and being encouraged by people like Trenton—men and women and boys and girls who are often marginalized, forgotten by society, exploited and used for profit or pleasure. I'm profoundly grateful that Trenton has parents who love him fiercely and speak truth into his life, along with a church family that champions his dreams. Yet, millions worldwide live without that support, remaining unseen and unheard. Many of them have not been treated with the royal dignity they were born with. Many of them don't even realize they have an inherent divine worth. And while society may have given up on them because it tends to see MVPs as inconsequential, their royal worth never changes.

We weren't called to bask in our royal status just for a confidence boost. As God's image, we are commanded to defend the weak, protect the poor, and pursue the hurting so they know that they, too, are God's image.

Part 2

RENEW YOUR

HOPE

IT'S NOT ABOUT WHETHER WE CONTRIBUTE TO SOCIETY OR MEET THE WORLD'S STANDARDS OF ACHIEVEMENT; OUR WORTH IS UNSHAKABLE BECAUSE IT'S GIVEN TO US BY GOD.

Chapter 8

JESUS IN THE MARGINS

IN 2015 I WAS PLAYING FOR THE PHILADELPHIA Eagles. Scratch that—I was *trying* to play for the Eagles (I say *trying* because I ended up getting cut later in the year, before the season officially began). In between training, lifting, and practices, the team often went through different kinds of tests. It was a way for the coaches and trainers to try to make us football players even just 1 percent better. I appreciated their dedication to our performance. During one eye exam, I noticed the doctor was unusually expressive, despite the protocol to keep findings under wraps until the assessment was complete. Every few seconds, he let out a thoughtful "hmm," each one growing longer and closer together. Finally, he looked up from his notes and asked, "So Timmy, how long have you known you're colorblind?"

My forehead wrinkled. "I'm sorry, what?"

"You didn't know?"

"That I was colorblind?" I've been told I was a lot of things over the years, but being colorblind was definitely not one of them.

"Oh yes," the doctor stated with a firm nod. "You're definitely colorblind."

The reality of this new diagnosis didn't really hit in the moment, but looking back it makes a pretty good excuse for all the interceptions I threw.

Colorblind? I had spent almost three decades on this earth without an inkling that I struggled to tell some colors apart, especially red and green, thanks to the way my eyes' cone cells process color. Most people don't even know they are colorblind until a doctor figures it out for them. Like me, they adapt without realizing it. What they see is what they see—until they get a chance to look again and realize what they've been missing.

A NEW LENS

I watched a video on YouTube of a man who was colorblind whose family recorded a video of him opening their birthday gift to him. He was in his mid-sixties and had a no-nonsense vibe, looking like the kind of guy who despised a birthday fuss and especially being filmed. True to form, he took his time opening the present. After he unwrapped his new pair of "sunglasses," someone behind the camera encouraged him to put them on. The man rolled his eyes and slipped on the glasses, unaware that they were meant to help illuminate certain colors he struggled to see. Suddenly, he froze. Then, gripping the sides of his new shades, he looked up. Then down. And real slow, side to side.

"How does it look?" the woman recording the video asked.

Barely above a whisper, the man replied, "Oh, that's weird."

"Do you see colors now?"

Lost in his new visual world, the man began to murmur to himself, lips barely moving. "The trees are green." His trembling hands clapped together as he continued to take in the world around him.

"Oh my. Oh wow. I've never seen this before," he said, his voice cracking.

Behind the camera, the woman began to sob, saying, "Now you can see with our eyes!"

Overwhelmed and speechless, the man fumbled with his pockets, like a four-year-old forced to wear a suit for the first time. The man's gaze darted in every direction, pausing every now and then to rest on vibrant green grass that once looked grayish and a rich blue sky he'd seen only in pale hues. Words failed him. Choked by sobs, he stood awestruck in the middle of a world he'd only just discovered. The man began to repeatedly slide the glasses down his nose and back up, over and over, switching from his view of the familiar muted world he knew to the vivid reality the new lenses introduced.

"Oh my goodness," he blurted. "Nothing looks like mud . . . The trees don't even look real. Seriously, they look 3D. I've never seen colors like that!" Gasping at every object revived in true colors for the first time, the man's fists clenched. He began pumping his arms, reminding me of another picture of a little kid, this time of one who just unwrapped the birthday present they'd always wanted but never believed they'd actually get. I can't help but tear up every time I watch that five-minute video.[1]

Over time, I processed what it meant to be colorblind. I wondered how often I have missed seeing something for what it really looked like. But the more I thought about it, the more another revelation came to light. This one deeper than seeing just color. How many times, I wondered, have I not seen *people* the way I should?

It's one thing to confuse my red and greens. It's another to make an unfair or unnecessary judgment about someone. There have been many times I've missed the mark in seeing people rightly because I'd seen them only through the lens of what they could do for me—by their talents, abilities, or how they might fit on a team—rather than valuing them simply for who they are.

Seeing ourselves as God sees us matters. But seeing others the same way God sees them matters too. Experiencing life with Jesus is like putting on glasses that transform how we see the world. Just as colorblind goggles may allow people to see the vivid beauty of colors they never knew existed, knowing Jesus and grounding ourselves in the truth that we are created as God's image should change how we see people.

GOD'S HEARTBEAT

Jesus has a profound ability to see beyond appearances and into the soul. Unlike us, He doesn't need to look again; He sees clearly the first time. It's no coincidence our Savior arrived on earth quietly, defying expectations as the opposite of the warrior king that some of the Jewish people anticipated. Over and over, He shattered people's assumptions and biases. Jesus wasn't born in a palace with gold floors but in a room with animals and their feed and excrement. Jesus didn't enter the world with fanfare but through scandal and the womb of an unknown and seemingly unremarkable teenage girl. Ancient scholars weren't present at His birth; common shepherds accepted the invitation.

When Jesus began His public ministry, He didn't announce his identity to the religious experts of the day or the Jerusalem morning show but to a woman from a different culture who had a checkered marital history. Jesus didn't surround Himself with an elite leadership team of sought-after speakers who had written multiple *New York Times* bestsellers but with a scrappy crew of men and women whose names had never made an A-list. Jesus' habit of regularly drawing near to lepers, dining with people of questionable company, standing up for the poor, and treating social pariahs with dignity was shocking to the customs of that time.

You could say that Jesus lived in the margins, what's defined as being "among the least typical or least important parts of" society or a group.[2] You know who occupies space in the margins? The MVP.

Jesus *sees* the marginalized; He sees their value. Isaiah 61 records a prophecy of the coming Messiah. Read the first verses:

> "The Spirit of the Sovereign Lord is on me, because the Lord has anointed me to proclaim good news to the poor. He has sent me to bind up the brokenhearted, to proclaim freedom for the captives and release from darkness for the prisoners, to proclaim the year of the Lord's favor and the day of vengeance of our God, to comfort all who mourn, and provide for those who grieve in Zion." (vv. 1–3)

Have you ever noticed who Jesus brought the good news to? While the obvious answer might be everyone—and that's true—this scripture in Isaiah specifically highlights vulnerable groups. Did you catch who's being described?

"the poor"
"the brokenhearted"
"the captives"
"the prisoners"
"all who mourn"
"those who grieve"

When I look at these descriptors, I don't think of the strong, powerful, and successful—at least not by society's standards. I think of people who live in the margins. The ones who struggle to fit in, to be seen, to be known. While a few cultures have esteemed people with disabilities—like the Dahomeans of West Africa, who believed that some babies born with special needs were seen as a sign of good luck or the Chagga of East Africa, who thought that children with disabilities appeased evil spirits, which would then protect the community from bad luck—most are looked down on.[3]

While Darwinism celebrates the strong as the ones who not only survive but also succeed, the Bible, through Jesus as God's ultimate image, shows up for the one who's alone, on the run, crushed, in darkness, chained, and in tears. If we want to know the heart of the Father, we look at the life of Jesus. What did Jesus do? He served, protected, and taught. He gave and helped. His attention was not just for the fancy or the fortunate.

> Jesus actively sought the MVP. And He still does.

Yes, Jesus actively sought the MVP. And He still does.

A PERSONAL AND TIMELESS BLUEPRINT

Theologian Narry Santos highlighted Jesus' servant heart toward the marginalized in an article drawing on sociological insights from the time when Mark's Gospel was written. In this Gospel, the marginalized refers to the poor, sick, leper, widow, wife, woman, child, and Gentile.[4] Seventy-five percent of the population consisted of commoners and farmers, such as fishermen, craftsmen, and slaves, while 10 percent were deemed "expendable," including beggars, the poor, prostitutes, and those with disabilities. Yet, Mark repeatedly showed Jesus seeking out, interacting with, uplifting, and healing people society decided were throwaways. Santos wrote,

As the essence of Jesus' ministry, servanthood is to be practiced by followers of Jesus on behalf of the marginalized—whether through a mighty act... or the giving of a cup of water... Moreover, servanthood is evident... by "becoming free to give oneself to others," especially for those who cannot give in return. Though it appears countercultural, having a humble heart actually commits the followers of Jesus to a life of service to other people who may appear to be of limited social significance.[5]

Jesus made it clear that serving the most vulnerable isn't just part of His mission; it is *personal* (Matthew 25). Jesus taught His disciples on the Mount of Olives about the end times and what really matters, describing the final judgment. He illustrated this moment by comparing it to a shepherd separating sheep from goats. The sheep represent people who show love and kindness to others by feeding the hungry, welcoming strangers, caring for the sick, and helping those in need.

The goats, on the other hand, represent those who ignore the needs of others. Their lack of compassion reveals their failure to truly love or serve God, and they are sent away. Jesus told how the King, who is really Himself, will say to the sheep, "Whatever you did for one of *the least of these* brothers and sisters of mine, you did for *me*" (Matthew 25:40). This illustration was more than a metaphor; it was deeply personal ("for me"). When someone feeds the hungry, welcomes a stranger, or comforts the broken, Jesus said they are actually doing those things for and to *Him*. He so closely identifies with the overlooked and hurting that their suffering becomes His suffering. Their care becomes His care. Their burdens, His own. What a beautiful picture of how much Jesus values those who society often forgets.

This illustration isn't meant to give us one more thing to check off our spiritual to-do list; it's there to show us that God's heart beats

> "Whatever you did for one of *the least of these* brothers and sisters of mine, you did for *me*." (Matthew 25:40)

for the weak, for the forgotten, and for the vulnerable. And to be more like Jesus—which is the goal for every believer—this is a meaningful step in that direction.

Whether serving the socially insignificant, religious and ethnic outsiders, or ostracized sinners, Jesus had a way of acknowledging the marginalized, elevating their status in His kingdom, and restoring their royal worth. He did this in three ways that may seem small at first glance but uncover the path to recognizing royal worth in others:

Jesus saw.

Jesus called people by name.

Jesus came close.

JESUS SAW

Throughout the Gospels, approximately sixty-seven times, Jesus is described as seeing specific people or situations.[6] For example, He saw Peter's mother-in-law lying in bed with a fever and healed her (Matthew 8:14–15). He watched the poor widow give two coins in the temple (Mark 12:41–42). He saw the woman who touched the fringe of His garment (Matthew 9:22). He saw the disabled man lying beside the pool of Bethesda (John 5:6). He saw the widow who had lost her only son, and then he raised him from the dead (Luke 7:13–15).

The writers of the Gospels emphasized Jesus as an observer. Much like the doctors who thoroughly examined us football players, He noticed everything—from spotting an individual in need to recognizing someone misusing their power. Nothing got past Jesus, especially the vulnerable. Not even shoulder-to-shoulder crowds where voices clashed at peak volume were a match for Jesus' willingness to see.

Mark 10 tells the story of Bartimaeus. About two weeks before Passover, when He would be killed, Jesus was walking along a road crowded with followers when a blind beggar called out: "Jesus, Son of David, have mercy on me!" (Mark 10:47). Viewing the man as nothing but a nuisance, the crowd started shushing him. As a blind beggar, Bartimaeus had a double burden that made him easy to marginalize. Those around Jesus made sure to remind him of this by trying to shush him up. But Bartimaeus wasn't the type to stay quiet. His persistence was probably an instinctive trait for someone who depended on the pity of others to survive.

It's remarkable when you think about it: Bartimaeus, being blind, had never witnessed any of Jesus' miracles firsthand. What he knew about Jesus was likely a mix of good and bad rumors. But deep down, he believed there was something extraordinary about Him. So, he cried out again, "Have mercy on me!" (v. 48).

Jesus' response is interesting. He didn't immediately say, "Hey there. Need my help to start seeing? Let's do this!" and—poof!—miraculously fix the blind beggar's vision problem. Jesus asked Bartimaeus, "What do you want me to do for you?" (v. 51). This tells us that Jesus did more than see this man. He saw beyond the disability people fixated on. Yes, the man's visual impairment was obvious. And he likely bore the signs of a hard life on the streets. But this overlooked man could "see" what others around him could not: the true identity of the Messiah!

In return, Jesus saw what others could not in Bartimaeus: a need deeper than the surface, deeper than others assumed needed fixing. Instead of assuming He knew what this man experiencing disability needed, Jesus gave the man free agency to speak from the heart and share what *he* felt was his greatest need. He didn't assume that everything broken, crooked, or messy had to be "fixed." Jesus looked past appearances and saw the man's true value.

JESUS CALLED PEOPLE BY NAME

Throughout the Gospels, many individuals are first identified by their sin, disability, ailment, or social status. But when they encounter Jesus, everything changes. While society tends to label and dismiss, Jesus calls by name, offering respect and restoring worth.

Take Mary Magdalene, who before meeting Jesus was possessed by seven demons. In her community, being known for having demonic influence was an open road to social stigma and ostracism. Mary was never nominated for any Women of the Year awards. And yet, after being delivered from evil and becoming a close follower of Jesus, she was the first one to whom Jesus appeared after His death and resurrection. This woman recognized Jesus only after He called her by name—"Mary."[7]

> While society tends to label and dismiss, Jesus calls by name, offering respect and restoring worth.

In Luke 19:2, 7, Zacchaeus is called a "chief tax collector" and a "sinner," labels akin to a community menace and manipulator. Short in stature, the guy had to scale a tree to try to get Jesus' attention. When Jesus caught the eyes of this sinner and tax collector, He said, "Zacchaeus, come down" and received him joyfully (vv. 5–6). And then as an added bonus, Jesus gave the honor of hospitality to the last person everyone would have expected—*Zacchaeus*. The crowd was so upset by Jesus' gesture that the text says they "grumbled" at the sight of it (v. 7 CEB).

In the ancient world, names were deeply tied to a person's identity, revealing who they were, where they came from, and to whom they belonged. Unlike today, when calling someone by name is often just a greeting reflex, in biblical times it carried a deeper meaning of identity. Saying someone's name reclaimed a sense of worth that was stripped away by societal prejudice. It recognized who someone was instead of reducing a person to a role, illness, or moral failure. It shattered social hierarchies put in place to value only the wealthy or religious. When Jesus called someone by name, He recognized their God-given value.

I'll never forget attending a weekend retreat led by Pastor Dave Stone and his wife, Beth. Dave had been there for only about an hour or two, having just met most of the seventy attendees for the first time. The night we arrived, he delivered a message about God calling us by name. When it was over, he did something that blew me away. He asked everyone to stand and then instructed us to sit once he called out our name. Then, without looking at any notes and keeping his eyes fixed on us, he started calling each attendee by name. I'd never seen anyone do that before! Pastor Dave, within just a short time of meeting most of us, remembered each of our names. To this day, people still talk about that moment.

Being called by name and not by wins or losses, abilities or deficits reinforces our worth and value.

JESUS CAME CLOSE

Jesus regularly broke social customs, such as coming close to lepers, deemed outcasts. Leprosy is a bacterial infection that attacks the peripheral nerves. In biblical times, it was regarded as a curse from God or a consequence of sin. While the Greek word *lepra* and the Hebrew word *tsara'ath* are commonly translated into English as "leprosy," back then it was actually a term that referred to a variety of skin diseases.[8]

Possibly contagious and believed to be incurable, leprosy was ranked as the second-most serious defilement according to Jewish law, just behind contact with a dead body.[9] Lepers had to wear tattered clothing, and if they approached people, they were required to warn them by yelling, "Unclean! Unclean!"[10] Jewish tradition suggests that the stigma was so severe that lepers were forbidden from coming within six feet of other people. On windy days, that distance expanded to a staggering one hundred feet.[11] The law didn't only impose physical separation; it forced lepers to leave their families, jobs, and communities entirely, condemning them to a life of isolation and misery. Lepers were basically cut off from living with others.

Luke 5 introduces us to a leper. The Bible doesn't tell us his name, but we can be sure that a man with this condition knew what it meant to be isolated, rejected, and forgotten. As soon as the leper saw Jesus, "he fell with his face to the ground and begged him, 'Lord, if you are willing, you can make me clean'" (Luke 5:12). Before Jesus answered, He came close to the leper. Gasps probably rippled through the crowd as He moved toward the sick man. But Jesus, willing, moved by deep compassion—literally stirred in the depths of His soul, as the Greek suggests[12]—broke societal norms without hesitation. He knelt on the ground, inches away from the leper sprawled in the dust. Unlike everyone else around Him, Jesus wasn't repulsed by the leper. He wasn't concerned with the disapproving whispers. He also wasn't scared of getting sick.

Squatting on the side of the road as some of the people likely warned Jesus to back up, Jesus moved closer. He "reached out his hand and touched the man. 'I am willing,' he said. 'Be clean!' And immediately the leprosy left him" (Luke 5:13).

The text says Jesus saw and then touched. What the text doesn't include but implies is that Jesus had to walk over to the disgraced man in order to touch him. He had to eliminate distance. Walk to him. I can almost hear the shouts from anyone within earshot. "Jesus, what are You doing? The guy has leprosy!" "Are You crazy? Stop!" "Come back already!"

Jesus wasn't intimidated or constrained by distance. With one foot in front of the other, He covered the ground between Him and the man with leprosy. He didn't have to draw near to the sick man. He could have healed the leper from miles away with just a word. Jesus covered the ground and came close because that's who He is. Closeness breeds connection. It transcends barriers. By coming close, Jesus showed the man he mattered—and reminded us to move toward people who are hurting.

Can any of us survive without closeness? Proverbs 18:14 reminds us not only to serve but to draw near, to console and uplift, for "the human spirit can endure in sickness, but a crushed spirit who can bear?" Kathy Berns, a mother in her seventies who cares for her adult son Jared, who has special needs, related just how important that is.

As of this writing, Jared is forty years old and has been neurologically impaired since birth. He lives with his mother and has a deep passion for life and staying active. His days are filled with activities like horseback riding, rowing, and surfing, thanks to local organizations supporting individuals with special needs. A dog lover, he also faithfully walks his neighbor's dog every day.

Despite his zest for life, Jared struggles with short-term memory and has never been able to express his emotions verbally. Kathy often wondered if it was due to his limited emotional capacity or an inability to articulate his feelings.

Like many others, Jared had a hard time with the isolation sparked by COVID in 2020. Unable to participate in the activities he loved, he grew frustrated, and the strain began to affect his relationship with Kathy, who struggled as his sole caregiver. Then, in 2021, the NTS drive-through event arrived.

Knowing the celebration would take place in a car line instead of the usual venue with dancing and karaoke, Kathy wasn't sure how Jared would react. But the moment they pulled into the church parking lot, both mother and son were stunned. Volunteers filled the space, stationed at six different stops. Some drew hearts with soap on car windows, while others waved colorful signs reading, You're Amazing! and You Are Loved! Cheers and applause erupted for every VIP guest. The physical surroundings of NTS may have looked different from previous years, but the vibe was the same.

"You could feel the love. It was undeniable," Kathy recalled.

Amid the celebration, Jared, unusually quiet, turned to his mother with tears streaming down his face. "Are they really here for me? Am I really that special?" he asked.

Kathy, tears welling in her own eyes, smiled and assured him, "Yes, they are here for you. And you really are that special."[13]

In that moment, Jared expressed something he never had before, and Kathy realized he had likely never felt love so deeply. The NTS volunteers had made him feel truly seen. It doesn't have to take big gestures to treat someone as God sees them. Take it from Jesus and just take a step forward. Start by coming close and recognizing how special they are.

LET IT RAIN

On June 2, 1953, twenty-seven-year-old Elizabeth II was crowned queen in a coronation ceremony at Westminster Abbey in London. My wife watched its historical dramatization in the Netflix series *The Crown*. Demi loves all things royal, and I've often seen her with a group of friends bingeing this series.

Steeped in religious tradition, historical significance, and lavish pageantry, the three-hour event was a display of opulence: from the Queen's top-secret gown, guarded by a policeman during its creation, to her gold carriage drawn by eight horses. A procession of 250 dignitaries, including church leaders, prime ministers, and military officials, entered the abbey, while 8,251 guests filled the audience.[14] The Queen wore not one but two crowns—one for the coronation ceremony and one for afterward—each crafted from gold and encrusted with diamonds, rubies, pearls, sapphires, and other precious gemstones.

For the first time in history, this iconic ceremony was televised. An estimated twenty-seven million Britons watched from their screens, while eleven million more tuned in by radio. Three million people gathered along the streets and sidewalks to catch a glimpse of the Queen and other dignitaries during the procession route from Buckingham Palace to Westminster Abbey and back. Some camped overnight, others for two days—much like today's Black Friday sales or Comic-Con crowds—to secure the best views.[15]

Though meteorologists had recommended June 2 as the day with the lowest forecast chance of rain, the weather did not cooperate. It rained. This wasn't a light drizzle but a true downpour, especially during the Queen's procession from the abbey back to the palace.[16] Most carriages, bearing heads of state and international figureheads, naturally closed their tops to protect their royal passengers from the elements. Except one.

In a moving display of honor and respect, Queen Salote Tupou III of Tonga rode in an open carriage, smiling and waving passionately despite being drenched. As one journalist noted, she looked "happy as though all the sun of the friendly islands were beating down."[17] The crowd roared with delight. Besides Queen Elizabeth herself and former Prime Minister Winston Churchill, this regal Polynesian leader stole the show. She captured the hearts of all who watched.

I can tell you from experience that standing, sitting, or doing anything in the rain for hours is not fun. I don't know anyone who would willingly endure that low-key agony if they didn't absolutely have to. Although to some, an NTS event may not hold as much weight as an actual royal coronation, we try to make each guest feel like a king or a queen. So, when we were in Brazil a few years ago and it started to rain in sheets right before our honored guests began showing up and heading down the red carpet, I started feeling bummed out.

When I didn't see many people looking for umbrellas to help our soon-to-arrive guests stay dry, my irritation grew. To make matters worse, as I looked around, I noticed some of our team and other volunteers were either safely tucked under awnings or doorways or sprinting to get there. Clearly, they did not want to get wet. And yet, in just a few minutes, our guests of honor would be getting soaked down the red carpet. That reality flipped a switch in me.

I wasn't irritated that people wanted to stay dry. I get that! Heck, I didn't want to be at the mercy of a downpour. The problem was that running and standing under an awning or a doorway sent a very loud and very clear message to our guests. Without saying a word, it signaled to them that they were less important than our comfort. And that is the opposite of what we aim to embrace at NTS.

As an athlete, I've learned that sometimes, in the heat of the moment, you get a chance to change the momentum, to make a statement that's about more than just yourself. I wasn't about to let a little rain shift our focus away from what mattered. It was time to press the reset button.

In a flash, while umbrellas were being fetched, the first car inched toward the red carpet. I jumped out of the line I was standing in and helped our first guest out of the car. Then, one of our team members stepped out from under the awning, clapping and cheering as the guest walked down the red carpet. One by one, more volunteers followed, holding umbrellas—not for themselves but for our guests. Soon, everyone lined the red carpet, cheering as hairdos were ruined, makeup ran, and fancy shoes splashed through puddles. But no one cared.

We were soaked, laughing, and having the time of our lives—because our guests were doing the same. It was a night none of us would ever forget. I remember watching two security guards who were with us. These men were trained to be focused, stoic, and unemotional. Not even a flinch could escape their posture. But then something changed in one man in particular. Something in the way he saw royalty in every individual on that soaked red carpet and the way love was shown cracked him on the inside. He stood in front of us, unable to control a tremble, which led to a full breakdown. As he sobbed, I watched God rip him open in the best kind of way. When you see people how God sees them, it's almost impossible to stay the same.

That rain-soaked red carpet experience in Brazil was a much-needed reminder that we are in charge of setting the tone. Tone is contagious. It can either ignite breakthrough or burn everything down. We may not have control over every situation, but we always have control over how we respond. No matter how chaotic things get, the tone we choose to set makes all the difference. It may be comfortable to stay dry. It may look and feel better too. But at the same time, it also sends a message that our needs, our preferences, our desires, and our reputation matter more than the people we are honoring on the red carpet. And that's just not right.

Queen Salote got it right that rainy June afternoon in 1953. She could have pulled the top of her carriage to be drawn up and over her. Nobody would have chastised her for doing it—everybody else was smiling and waving from the shelter of their own covered carriages. But knowing millions had come to see this royal parade, the queen of Tonga wasn't about to let a little rain stop her from seeing them—and them from seeing her. She carried herself with a deep sense of responsibility as royalty, as if thinking, *If the people are out here getting drenched, then I can be too.* It wasn't about superiority but about embracing her role as a royal representative—leading by example rather than seeking comfort. Queen Salote understood a truth that should resonate with all of us: True royalty isn't about comfort or indulgence; it's about responsibility and stewardship.

Chapter 9

GOD'S IMAGE—NO EXCEPTIONS

MARTIN OATES, A CIVIL WAR SOLDIER, RETURNED to San Francisco paralyzed after an injury forced his discharge from the army. Unable to work, Martin resorted to begging on the streets. In July 1867, *The San Francisco Morning Call*, a local newspaper, reported his arrest, describing Martin as a "poor, half demented fellow" and a "perfect wreck."[1] Martin was the first person in San Francisco and in the United States to become a target of an ordinance to "Restrict Certain Persons from Appearing in Streets and Public Places."[2] Though intended to curb street begging, this law included provisions specifically aimed at people with disabilities.[3] Here's exactly what it said:

> Any person who is diseased, maimed, mutilated, or in any way deformed so as to be an unsightly or disgusting object, or an improper person to be allowed in or on the streets, highways . . . or public places in the City or County of San Francisco, shall not . . .

expose himself or herself to public view. Any person who shall violate the provisions of this section shall be deemed guilty of a misdemeanor; and on conviction thereof, shall be punished by a fine not exceeding twenty-five dollars, or by imprisonment in the county jail not exceeding twenty-five days, or by both such fine and punishment.[4]

Sparking a "civic contagion" in the next few decades, other metropolitan cities like Portland, Chicago, and Denver followed suit.[5] These municipalities adopted language similar to San Francisco's ordinance, enacting laws to criminalize people considered "diseased, maimed, mutilated, or in any way deformed"[6]—what would later be coined in 1975 as the "ugly laws."[7]

JUDGED UNFIT FOR THE PUBLIC EYE

While these laws had several motivations, their primary aim was to remove individuals with visible physical disabilities from public view, deeming them an eyesore.[8] As a New Orleans paper put it, "Street begging is confessedly a great nuisance, but when it is joined . . . with the exposure of deformities, disease, and sores, it is simply unendurable."[9] A journalist from New York City said it bluntly, "When you are on your way to dinner, or to visit your beloved, or have composed in your mind the last stanza of the new poem that has given you such trouble, it is not agreeable to be confronted by some loathsome vision."[10]

Chicago implemented its own ugly law in 1881, similar to San Francisco, but reduced the fine from as much as twenty-five dollars to just one dollar. Arrested offenders with disabilities were detained at the police station before being transferred to an almshouse, which at the time was a public institution that housed the poor and disabled, deliberately erasing them from public spaces.[11] James Peevey, the government official who implemented this particular law, was hailed by a local paper as a "public benefactor" for removing a woman who, despite losing her job to a workplace injury, resorted to musical street performances with her two sick children to survive.[12]

In 1911, the Midwestern city amplified the ordinance's impact to include people who exposed "diseased, mutilated, or deformed portions of the body," such as missing limbs. The city upped the ante again later that same year with an additional addendum. This modification banned people "whose deformity is such as to excite public curiosity."[13]

These laws may have been influenced by what seemed to be a public outcry as recorded in newspapers. One article noted that seeing someone with "repulsive deformity" may pose a danger to "a lady in delicate health." Another condemned the obstruction of a thoroughfare by people with special needs, what they referred to as "hideous monstrosities, which are only half human."[14] This dehumanizing mindset worked its way through the legal system throughout the country, calling for the arrest of people like a young man from Cleveland, Ohio, with clubbed hands and clubbed feet in the early 1910s. In 1916, he unjustly lost the job that was supporting both himself and his family: selling, of all things, newspapers—the very outlet that was being used to spurn his existence.[15]

By the early 1970s, some cities still had the ugly laws on their books.[16] In 1974, Chicago finally abolished the last of them. A co-sponsor of the repeal aptly described it as "cruel and insensitive . . . a throwback to the Dark Ages."[17]

More than a century after the passage of the initial ugly laws, while legislation has made great strides in advocating for people with special needs, I often wonder what our hearts—not just our words—truly say about them. We may no longer campaign to remove the vulnerable from public view, but do we acknowledge the worth of individuals who are neurologically and physically impaired?

How might the lives of MVPs—and our own—transform if we recognized every person as God's image, imbued with royal worth? I don't have an exact answer, but I do know that if we chose to see as God sees and to value others as He does, perhaps we wouldn't receive so many heartbreaking letters like this one from our partner in Uganda—messages we receive far too frequently.

> Persons with disabilities are often stigmatized and discriminated against in their families and communities. There is often false information, false assumption, and an incomplete understanding of God's design and purpose for their life. When a parent or caregiver is told that their child has a disability, they can be overcome with feelings of disbelief, anxiety, fear, depression, or shame. Some may also ask questions of "why me" and conclude that they are being punished for sins or bad acts of the past. Depending on the severity of the disability and the magnitude of the demand for coping, a few parents may even contemplate death for the child or themselves. We have even heard . . . "My child is a burden, and they have no place in my family . . . I have three kids, but one doesn't count."

I can almost hear God's heart breaking over these words—the anguish, the sorrow, the pain of a world that devalues the worth of people with disabilities and believes they don't count in God's roll call. Everything in Scripture—from humankind as being fearfully and wonderfully made and the finished work of the cross—screams the opposite. No one is overlooked. No one is forgotten. And if every life counts with Him, every life should count with us.

Sixteen percent of the world's population (1.3 billion people or 1 in 6) are reported to have significant disabilities.[18] The Ugly Laws sought to erase such people from public view, describing them as "loathsome," "half human," or "repulsive," and shipping them off to institutions.[19] Sterilization legislation aimed to extinguish the possibility of babies with special needs from being born. Euthanasia programs systemically killed children, men, and women deemed burdens on society, families, and the government.

And while people with disabilities were and still are treated as less than human, others have been oppressed for the color of their skin. People of color have been enslaved, segregated, and crushed under the weight of Jim Crow laws. All these laws we've talked about in this book (and so many others) reflect deeply flawed beliefs that human definitions of worth and usefulness supersede the status of royal worth God has stamped on the identity of each person. When we judge others through a limited lens, we set up a flawed picture. But God views each human being through a different lens. With this divine vision, He sees every person as fearfully and wonderfully made.

MORE THAN MEETS THE EYE

Baby S's story began in the most heartbreaking way. Abandoned in the bush at birth, the placenta was still connected to his body when he was found. Baby S began his life alone, vulnerable, and near death. It seemed the world had written him off, but in that moment of darkness, the Lord was watching. In His infinite grace, Baby S was found, rescued, and brought into the care of those who would love him deeply. Though his beginning was humble, his story was far from over—it was just the beginning of a great transformation.

As Baby S grew, something became undeniably clear—this child, who was once left for dead, carried something royal inside of him. The people who cared for him didn't only see where he came from—they saw who he was created to be. And so did God. The Master Story Maker was rewriting Baby S's narrative, turning brokenness into beauty, and offering him a future that was bright with promise. He is living proof that the Lord can take any story—no matter how broken—and transform it into something royal, filled with love, worth, and unshakable purpose.

Humans have a natural tendency to measure worth based on what meets the eye, or what we see on the surface. We see this in Scripture when God directed the prophet Samuel to anoint Saul's successor as king, leading him to the house of Jesse. When Samuel arrived and began to inspect the lineup of brothers, his inclination was to pick the firstborn, Eliab. Not only the oldest but the first to catch the prophet's eye, Eliab was likely tall, strong, and handsome. But God stopped Samuel in his tracks. Surprisingly, this strapping specimen wasn't the right guy for the job. God told Samuel, "Do not consider his appearance or his height, for I have rejected him. The LORD does not look at the things people look at. People look at the outward appearance, but the LORD looks at the heart" (1 Samuel 16:7).

The Lord does not look at the things people look at. Or as another translation puts it, "God *sees* not as man sees" (NASB). Thank God for His divine vision! Unfortunately, the Bible is full of examples in which, contrary to the heart of God, MVPs with disabilities were devalued by a human lens. Let's look back at Mephibosheth. His words were a self-imposed condemnation when he called himself a "dead dog" (2 Samuel 9:8). How about the man lying by the pool of Bethesda who had been paralyzed for decades? This man, often overlooked and ignored, received no help from bystanders when he tried getting into the pool for healing (John 5). Consider the man born blind who was encountered by Jesus and His disciples; the first question the disciples asked Jesus about this man was whether his blindness resulted from his parents' sin.

Our royal status as God's image comes from the intrinsic value He placed on each and every human being from the very beginning. I can't stress this enough: It's not about whether we contribute to society or meet the world's standards of achievement; our worth is unshakable because it's given to us by God.

Demi's sister Franje was born with a rare condition called cerebellar agenesis, where the brain forms without a cerebellum. My sister-in-law passed away at just thirteen years old, never having the chance to talk, walk, feed herself, brush her hair, tell her parents she loved them, play dress-up with Demi, or pet a dog. Her status as God's image wasn't diminished by what she could or couldn't do. From the moment she was knit together in her mother's womb to the day she entered heaven's gates, her worth remained the same—royalty.

Let's never confuse worth with impact. Yes, some people will inspire, challenge, or bring millions to Christ through the reach of their platform. But their value is no greater than that of the MVP whose life is confined to a bed, their only function battling for breath. Worth isn't earned—it's given by God, equally and unconditionally. His royal imprint is stamped on the DNA of every person, even those dismissed by medical experts as unworthy of life.

> Let's never confuse worth with impact.

AGAINST ALL ODDS

"The best thing to do for everyone involved is to terminate your pregnancy," the doctor told six-month-pregnant Stacie, one of our amazing NTS host church coordinators. A routine ultrasound had revealed that her baby, Jacob, had spina bifida, a birth defect in which the spine is incompletely developed. In early pregnancy, a set of cells forms what's called a neural tube. The top part becomes the brain and the rest become the spinal cord and the bones around it. With spina bifida, which means "split spine," the tube doesn't close all the way, resulting in physical challenges and potential learning disabilities.

Jacob also had hydrocephalus, extra fluid in and around the brain. Before the doctor recommended Stacie abort Jacob, the doctor described the miserable life that her baby would have if he were born. "He will probably not see or hear. He won't talk. He'll probably be a vegetable."

As Stacie's world began to spin out of control, she was sure of one thing that she made clear to the doctor: "This is my son, and we will not be terminating his life." In 1997, the internet didn't exist in most households, so Stacie and her husband at the time spent countless hours in medical libraries learning everything they could about spina bifida. What they read wasn't promising. Most of Stacie's research suggested that as many as 80 percent of babies with the condition die at birth.

Jacob was born at thirty-eight weeks via scheduled C-section on June 16. Before he was six hours old, he had two surgeries. One to close his back and another to insert a shunt to drain the fluid in his brain, relieving pressure. Things seemed okay and Jacob was even able to come home, but not for long. At two weeks old, he developed breathing issues called stridor, a condition his doctor earlier warned Stacie was possible but rare. Over the next few weeks, doctors performed a variety of surgeries.

When he was just eight weeks old, Jacob underwent a high-risk surgery to create more space for his brainstem. The likelihood of success was low: a one-in-three chance he wouldn't survive, a one-in-three chance it would fix the problem, and a one-in-three chance it would do nothing. The latter outcome proved true. The surgery did nothing and Jacob needed a tracheostomy to keep breathing, a surgery that creates a hole in the neck through which a tube is inserted, enabling breathing directly through the windpipe. This wasn't a temporary fix; Jacob would need it for the rest of his life. He also developed sleep apnea and needed a ventilator whenever he slept and a misting machine when he was awake so his lungs wouldn't dry out.

Jacob's care in his early life was complex and grueling, requiring around-the-clock supervision. He was four months old when he came home from Tucson Medical Center for good, the youngest person ever to come out of there with a ventilator. Before Jacob was discharged, his parents had to complete a two-day training session at the hospital, proving they could take care of their baby's needs. Stacie remembers sitting in the meeting with a friend and a room full of twenty doctors, nurses, and staff days before Jacob would come home. The hospital staff took turns asking questions to ensure the baby's parents had everything they needed to keep Jacob safe and secure.

Suddenly, Stacie raised her hand. "I know his ventilator has a travel battery, but the rest of Jacob's equipment requires electricity. What will we use to power his equipment when we are out and about?"

It was as if her question sucked the air out of the room. After a few seconds of stunned silence, the pulmonologist spoke up. "I'm sorry, but where exactly are you planning on going with this child?"

Stacie blinked slowly. "Uh, church. His grandmother's house.

The zoo. The park and any other places people normally take their babies—."

Shaking her head, the pulmonologist interrupted. "Under no circumstances is this child allowed to go anywhere for the next year."

"I don't understand," Stacie protested. "Why did we work so hard to fight for Jacob to have life if we're just going to keep him at home every day? That doesn't make sense!"

No one said a word in response. Determined, Stacie believed otherwise. *There must be another way.* Jacob's fragility was monitored at home, day and night, by his family and night nurses. As he got older, Jacob required a wheelchair that he would need for the rest of his life. When he was about ten years old, he began to experience chronic pain, likely due to nerve damage, which became a struggle in his later years. He also suffered from blacking out episodes, during which his vascular system would essentially freeze, leaving him unresponsive for several minutes.

Despite his physical limitations, constant medical challenges, difficulty breathing, and more than eighty-five surgeries throughout his lifetime, Stacie and her family committed to making sure they would never restrict Jacob from living a full life beyond medical appointments, physical therapy, and surgeries. And that he did. Jacob went to school with the other kids in the community and made lasting friendships. He enjoyed roller coasters, loud concerts, and many family vacations to the mountains and to the beach. Perhaps most inspiring, every day he'd ask whoever he would see how they were and how he could help. Stacie put it this way: "Jacob, the boy who couldn't even scratch his own nose, just wanted to bless and do for us every day—and he did."

Jacob's final years were marked by severe pain and several medical crises. One day, after being episode-free for a long time, Jacob blacked out and had to be hospitalized. On March 29, 2017, at 8:32 p.m., Stacie held her beloved son in her arms as he was ushered into heaven to be with Jesus forever.

A few years earlier, one of Stacie's friends experienced the loss of her young daughter in a drowning accident. At the funeral of the little girl, Jacob approached the grieving mother and said, "I just want you to know that I'll probably be in heaven before you. I'll make sure to take care of Olivia for you." Stacie is certain Jacob is now fulfilling that promise. She also pictures him living out another cherished dream—finally racing with Jesus with his new body.

ALWAYS A DIAMOND

Stacie will tell you today that she has no regrets. As she put it:

> We didn't always parent perfectly, but we loved Jacob fiercely. We fought for the life we wanted him to have . . . This isn't a pat on our backs. It's a standing ovation to our precious God who, in His divine goodness, gave us Jacob and equipped us for the journey. God gave us miracles every step of the way. Time and again, we were told what Jacob couldn't or wouldn't do—and then he did, defying the impossible.

These words spoken about Jacob are not just inspiring but should encourage us that "broken" bodies do not hold power to diminish the value God has placed in them. What's also true is that some MVPs don't live as long or have severe physical and mental impairment that prevent them from experiencing certain activities. Yet, God's worth remains unchanged. Franje's worth was neither diminished nor enhanced by the fact that she never walked a step or spoke a word in her life. Our image is not based on how motivating or limiting our stories are. God declares the same royal value over every life.

Imagine walking along a gravel path, kicking up pebbles with every step. They're tiny. Common. Easily overlooked. Most of us don't stop to pick one up—it's just a pebble, insignificant, forgettable. And if for some reason you do pocket one, chances are by the end of the day, you won't even remember it's there.

Now, imagine a glint of light catching your eye. You reach down and pick up what looks like just another pebble. But as you brush away the dirt, you realize—it's a diamond. Your eyes widen. Your heart races. In that moment, time seems to pause. Suddenly, what was once ordinary is now priceless. Rare. Irreplaceable. And because of its value, you treat it differently. You treasure it. You protect it.

How often do we mistake diamonds for pebbles? In our busyness, distractions, and preoccupations, we walk past people—barely noticing them, barely acknowledging their worth. Society conditions us to believe that some lives matter more than others, that some people are disposable, that their suffering isn't our concern. But the only difference between a pebble and a diamond is the lens through which you see it.

God never mistakes a diamond for a pebble.

> God never mistakes a diamond for a pebble.

Some people have been told their entire lives that they are just pebbles—common, replaceable, worth nothing more than to be kicked aside. But when we see them through God's eyes, through the lens of His love, everything changes. He sees people exactly as they are—precious, irreplaceable, worth the life, death, and resurrection of His Son, Jesus.

Instead of treating diamonds like pebbles, together let's strive to see people the way God sees them. See yourself the way God sees you. Because when you do, you won't just walk past someone again—you'll walk toward them. You'll love differently. You'll live differently. And that changes everything.

Chapter 10

ROYALTY IN RUBBLE

> ****WARNING****
>
> This section contains potentially triggering subject matter including examples of sexual and physical abuse and may be difficult to read due to its graphic nature. It is not shared for gratuitous purposes but to unmask the depths of evil, shedding light on the ways such behavior manipulates, distorts, and seeks to destroy the intrinsic worth of human beings as God's image.
>
> *All names of survivors mentioned have been changed to protect their privacy.

OUR MISSION AT THE FOUNDATION IS TO BRING faith, hope, and love to those needing a brighter day in their *darkest hour of need*. The last part of that sentence means different things to the people we serve. For us, sometimes it means confronting a shocking depth of darkness, the kind that rattles your soul to brutal realities you cannot unsee.

DARKEST HOUR OF NEED

God's image is being abused for the ultimate purpose of destroying the soul. This is what I call royalty in rubble, the reality of how humanity can turn on its own kind, on God's own image, in the most horrific and debased ways.

Across the world—in both wealthy nations and impoverished ones, in neighborhoods that celebrate with block parties and those torn apart by war, in families that send cheerful Christmas cards and those ripped apart by dark secrets—children, men, and women endure unimaginable horrors.

What does someone's darkest hour of need truly look like? Often, it stretches far beyond a single hour. It spans days, months, or even years of relentless physical, mental, and emotional abuse. It's reflected in the stories of lives brought out from the very edge of despair and depravity. Stories like that of a three-month-old baby with Down syndrome who was sexually abused. It looks like Dao, who fled a home where she was violently abused physically and sexually. After trusting a young man who promised her work at a karaoke bar, Dao was forced to have sex with customers and was trapped in trafficking for three years. It's the story of fourteen-year-old Lexi, who was sold for the equivalent of sixty dollars, only to endure two years of brutal forced labor in a meatpacking factory before being brought into freedom by a counter–human trafficking team.

These are categories of exploitation that are the end result of failing to see others according to their true worth. And they are evil. I believe that human trafficking (the act of forcing or coercing people into sex, labor, marriage, servitude, or even the removal of organs across various industries, both legal and illegal[1]) is one of the greatest evils we face today. Trafficking and related forms of exploitation affect nearly fifty million people a day.[2] In the United States, sex trafficking is the most prevalent form.[3] Children are especially vulnerable, making up 35 percent of all identified victims.[4] Experts believe this number reflects only a small portion of the many children who remain unidentified and unprotected.

Trafficking is a big business. According to the International Labour Organization, it brings in an estimated $236 billion in profit per year, $50.8 billion of which comes from child victims.[5] How much money is that? In football math, you could buy all thirty-two NFL teams, valued as of this writing at $190 billion, and still have a ton of cash left over.[6]

When people think of trafficking, they often imagine dramatic kidnappings, but most cases don't look like that. In reality, traffickers are usually someone the victim knows—romantic partners, parents, or other family members. In fact, 84 percent of victims are recruited by someone familiar, and 41 percent of child trafficking cases involve a family member.[7] Traffickers prey on the vulnerable—those who've experienced abuse, have disabilities, or face insecurity—and use manipulation, coercion, and fear in a slow, calculated process called grooming. It's not just strategic; it's evil.

Another devastating evil is the sexual exploitation and abuse of minors, an issue that threatens more than four hundred million children worldwide every year.[8] Behind that number are faces, real boys and girls who are being groomed, manipulated, and used in ways that are almost too heartbreaking to speak out loud. Some are targeted online by predators pretending to be someone they're not, what we call online enticement. Others are blackmailed into sharing images of themselves, a growing crime called sextortion.

And then there's the darkest layer: the production and trading of CSAM (child sexual abuse material). For those unfamiliar with that term, let me put it plainly: CSAM is photo or video evidence of children being sexually abused. Infants. Toddlers. Teens. Their pain, their trauma, is recorded and distributed like some sort of collectible—traded like baseball cards on hidden corners of the internet and sometimes in plain sight.

Camille Cooper, our VP of Human Trafficking and Child Exploitation at the foundation, has been fighting this battle for more than twenty years. Not long after she joined our team, I sat down with her and asked, "Camille, what breaks your heart the most?"

She stood up, walked over to the whiteboard in our office, and wrote one number: 20,000.

I stared at it for a second. "Twenty thousand what?" I asked.

Her answer still wrecks me.

"Twenty thousand unidentified boys and girls."

She explained that Interpol holds a massive international database filled with images and videos of children being abused. Then she shared shocking findings about this database: (1) More than 60 percent of unidentified victims are under twelve; (2) 47 percent contained extreme abuse, including torture and defecation; and (3) 4.3 percent of the images were of infants.[9] At the time, they estimated at least twenty thousand of those victims hadn't even been identified. No names. No rescues. No justice. Just lost kids stuck in digital evidence, waiting for someone to find them.

That moment changed something in us. We knew we had to respond. We couldn't unsee it, and we couldn't ignore it. That moment led to meetings, operations, and, eventually, action in the form of Operation Renewed Hope, what we have been told is one of the largest and most successful victim identification operations in the history of victim ID led by Homeland Security Investigations. To date, 1,119 children have been tentatively identified through Operation Renewed Hope I, II, and III.

More than three hundred have been safeguarded so far around the world (this number is probably not representative of actual survivors, as many agencies around the world are not always reporting numbers back to the United States). One case led to the identification of more than thirty other victims. We are so grateful to law enforcement as well as our partners for identifying and rescuing these children.

The darkness Camille unveiled pushed us to say, "God, use us. We're not fully prepared, but we're willing." Because this fight isn't just about stopping crime; it's about restoring value to God's most precious creation: people.

In March 2024, I had the incredible opportunity to testify in front of Congress along with Camille to increase awareness, foster collaboration with national and international agencies, and enhance legal measures to help safeguard vulnerable children and provide support to those affected by CSAM. We tried to give the United States government a clear message that day: Society must confront these challenging issues head-on. That morning, I woke up to a voice memo from one of the incredible survivors we have the honor of caring for. She was thanking us for speaking up—for her and for others like her. Being a voice for the voiceless is just one part of a much larger mission: fighting for those who can't fight for themselves. This precious survivor shared these words:

> When I was seven years old, I became a victim of online sexual exploitation of children. My family knew all that has happened to me. They let me participate and do indecent things at my young age. I was surrounded by people who were willing to hurt me. They used me for the sake of money to buy the things we needed. During these times, I was thinking of doing something bad to myself, maybe hurting myself or ending my life because I didn't know whether

what I was doing was right or wrong. What I was doing made my family happy, and I was doing it for them and for the money. I felt like I was standing in the middle of the fire, and no one would ever rescue me. But people came, helped and rescued me from all the people around me that wanted to hurt me . . . I'm so thankful because they loved me and cared for me without asking anything in return. In this home, I came to know God and His plans for my life . . . I found hope and peace and God is telling me. . . . I am not alone, He will never let me be hurt again and He will protect me always.[10]

She is one of the reasons we will continue to fight against child abuse and exploitation.

I was listening to author and speaker Dr. Frank Turek recently, and something he said really stuck with me. He explained that in his opinion evil isn't something in and of itself; it's the absence of good, the absence of God.[11]

If that's what evil is, then how many times have I contributed to it, not by what I've done but by what I've walked past? How many times have I chosen silence over discomfort? How often have I seen the devaluing of human life and just kept moving?

There's a lot of responsibility in recognizing that this world is filled with what God calls valuable, people made as His image, crowned with royal worth. You see, we all should recoil from evil like this and work to expose and destroy it. But we all also have our own repenting to do of the ways (most of which are far less heinous but still are serious) in which we don't act like other people are people. It's our job both to fight this evil as it seeks to engulf the vulnerable and the young *and* to ask, What in *ourselves* needs to be examined and brought to God? This is fighting the roots of evil where it starts—in the human heart. And it will begin to unlock the life of joy, victory, and unconditional love into which Jesus invites each one of us.

Every person who was and will ever be born *is* created in God's image—uniquely, beautifully, and perfectly, not to be sold or exploited for profit or pleasure. If I could talk to every boy or girl, man or woman who has been coerced, groomed, and conditioned to believe that trafficking, abuse, and exploitation is normal or something that they deserve, I would try to help them recognize and understand that their worth is infinite. It's woven into the fabric of their being because they are made as God's image. If they could even grasp just a fraction of that truth, it would change everything. If they could see themselves even slightly through God's eyes, through the way He created them, the love He demonstrated for them since the beginning of time, the sacrifice He made for them on the cross, it would shake the foundation of lies they have been told.

The reality that millions of people remain trapped in abusive circumstances is often hard for us to comprehend. Hell on earth, as real as it may be for these individuals, often seems overwhelming and beyond intervention to us on the outside. But God. With Him, all things are possible (Matthew 19:26). There is nothing so dark that His light cannot reach, no circumstances He cannot change, no people His love cannot rescue.

How it must break God's heart, over and over again, to see the crown of His creation ravaged by people who also carry His image. Every life has inherent value, even those who commit horrific acts. If you're like me, you'll admit this is a difficult truth to accept. However, the truth remains that all of us are God's image. All means all, including offenders, so much that Jesus died for them too. While we should not condone any evil action, and personal boundaries are necessary, we can acknowledge their worth as God sees it, hoping that through His love they might one day be transformed.

DARKNESS DEVALUES

The world is full of things that degrade and devalue human life. And if we don't realize that we, and everyone else, are created as God's image, we start to lose sight of what matters most—people.

So why am I telling you this? Because what we're up against is more than just injustice. Because we need to talk about what happens when we stop seeing people the way God sees them.

This isn't just about trafficking or child exploitation. It's about something deeper. It's about the devaluing of humanity. And it's everywhere. In the stories we ignore. In the needs we scroll past. In the kids who get laughed at because they look or speak differently. In the people we overlook because it's easier than engaging. It's in our everyday lives when we fail to honor the worth of the people around us.

Every life has royal worth. That's not just a feel-good phrase, that's truth. And it should drive how we see people, treat people, and fight for people. When we understand our own worth, we begin to recognize that same worth in others. And when we don't, we risk walking right past what's most precious to God.

I'm not suggesting that you become an expert in global issues. I'm saying that when God's creation is being torn down, we don't get to stay on the sidelines. Whether it's a child being exploited or a classmate being ignored, when we choose not to see, we choose not to value. And that choice matters.

Because to God, every person is priceless.

HOPE RENEWED

Stories of royalty in rubble can feel overwhelming, but they also ignite a powerful picture. I cannot imagine enduring the trauma these survivors have experienced. They are my heroes. I'll never forget baptizing a trafficking survivor for the first time. It happened a few years ago on a beach, during an already deeply emotional celebration. Surrounded by others there to support her, she turned to me and said, "Will you baptize me?" I felt honored, nervous, and overwhelmed all at once. This wasn't just another baptism; it was a sacred moment of healing and redemption. Baptizing a survivor carries a weight that's hard to describe. It's not just about water; it's about acknowledging their pain, honoring their journey, and witnessing the beauty of their redemption.

The gravity of it wasn't lost on me. I knew this act didn't save this young woman; salvation had already taken place in her heart through Jesus. But baptism is a public declaration of an inward transformation, and being part of that moment felt like holy ground. There's something powerful about letting others celebrate with you, about standing in front of witnesses and proclaiming what's already true in your heart. In that moment, you're part of something eternal, something beautiful, something that reminds us of the unshakable truth: God rescues, restores, and redeems.

What struck me most that day was how this moment symbolized both freedom from trafficking and freedom in Christ. I remember thinking, *This is exactly how it's supposed to be.* God had orchestrated this moment perfectly. Whether it's one survivor or a group of five on the beach, each baptism feels like a celebration of God's power to redeem and restore. It's also a welcome reminder of who our King is and what He has done for and in us.

Psalm 34:18 reminds us of where God can always be found—not

solely in grand temples, church buildings, or Christian concerts (though He is present there too), but especially with the brokenhearted and those crushed in spirit. Victims and survivors of trafficking, CSAM, and other evils know well that devastating place. They've described their pain to us using words like *traumatized, exhausted, sad, anxious, angry, numb, confused, alone,* and *afraid.* They've described waking from relentless nightmares, battling PTSD, wetting the bed out of fear, and struggling to form new bonds or relationships. The physical, emotional, and mental wounds they carry reflect a crushing brokenness that God comes close to and can begin to heal. Healing comes in many different forms, but the greatest comes from God.

> Psalm 34:18 is not just a promise to watch God draw near to the brokenhearted; it is a call for us to do the same.

Psalm 34:18 is not just a promise to watch God draw near to the brokenhearted; it is a call for us to do the same. If God is near the brokenhearted, then that is where we should be.

STEP INTO THE FRONT LINES

"That's not really my thing."

"I don't get involved in that kind of stuff."

I hear that a lot, and I get it! Not everyone is called to fight the evils of trafficking or CSAM. You can't be on every battlefield. But here's what I know for sure: Doing nothing isn't an option.

I remember one moment that still stays with me. We were driving through downtown Jacksonville. I saw a girl on the side of the road who looked lost and afraid. I stopped the car, got out, tried to encourage her, and gave her a book. I didn't realize it at the time, but she was being trafficked. Eventually she came into our ministry care and told us how that book had become her one thread of hope until her trafficker took it away. I didn't even know what that small moment meant until someone told me about it some time later. That's the thing: You don't have to do everything; you just have to do something.

You might not feel equipped. You might think, *That's not my gift*, or *I'm not trained for this*. But God has placed something in your hands. Use your voice. Use your skills. Use your time. Use your business. Use your platform. Not everyone is called to kick down doors and rescue kids, but everyone is called to value what God values.

This could mean mentoring a teen in your neighborhood, showing kindness to someone who's been overlooked, or leveraging your platform—whatever size it is—to speak up for people who don't have one. No matter what field you're in—you're in the right fight. The only question is: Which one are you going to choose? You don't have to start a nonprofit or move overseas. You just need to be faithful with what's in front of you.

Recently I was encouraging new entrepreneurs at a conference. I reminded them that success isn't just about return on investment, it's about return on impact. Scripture says, "Whatever your hand finds to do, do it with all your might" (Ecclesiastes 9:10). So do it. Build the business. Chase the dream. But don't make it just about money. Make it about people.

I've seen what happens when people let their platform become their purpose. I've seen entrepreneurs fight evil, create jobs, and use their influence to shift culture. But I've also seen people say the right things . . . and still do nothing. A good friend of mine presented a powerful opportunity to a company—one that could have safeguarded millions of children. But the company refused to even consider the proposal because it would impact their bottom line. In choosing inaction, they made their priorities clear: profit over children.

So no, you may not be called to fight trafficking. But don't say the cost is too high. Don't stand on the sidelines. Don't separate your purpose from your platform.

We don't get to look away.

We don't get to stay silent.

We do get to show up, right where we are, and use what we've been given to fight for what matters.

Because people matter.

And God's already made it clear: They're worth everything.

> We do get to show up, right where we are, and use what we've been given to fight for what matters.

FIGHTING *FROM* VICTORY

Confronting a darkness that distorts, devastates, and destroys God's image feels daunting most of the time. The kind of abuse I talked about may seem so unimaginable and all-consuming that it often leads to a painful pattern of looking away. Rather than engage and learn more about the stories of victims and survivors who have experienced hell on earth, we leave it to experts like governments, policy enforcers, or agencies that have the resources to do something about it.

But as believers, we are more capable of battling evil than we may think. God is bigger than crisis, conflict, and chaos. Across the world, He is rescuing and redeeming lives, shining light in dark places, even this very moment. Statistics might tell us we are losing the war on trafficking and exploitation—and frankly, we are—but God's Word reminds us that darkness will not have the final say. That's why we fight. It's why I hope I won't ever give up.

There is a tension in the battle we're fighting, and it's this: We are not fighting *for* victory; we are fighting *from* victory. That means we know how this ends. Jesus has won; therefore, as believers, so have we. The Enemy has been defeated. But that doesn't mean the punches or the bullets aren't real. That doesn't mean the wounds don't hurt and the scars don't last. That doesn't mean the stakes aren't high.

> We are not fighting *for* victory; we are fighting *from* victory.

The mission isn't about securing the win; it's about rescuing as many people as possible before time runs out. It's about pushing forward because, even though we know the outcome, there are still people who need to be rescued.

That's why we fight. That's why we press forward—not with fear, not with uncertainty, but with fire in our hearts. With confidence. With urgency. With passion. Because we know we're on the winning side. Now it's about making sure the Enemy doesn't take one more life than he already has.

As part 2 of this book ends, I hope your eyes have been opened, much like the man who first saw the world's vivid hues through colorblind glasses. The evil I've shared—human trafficking, sexual exploitation, and the mistreatment of those with special needs—represents just a fraction of the darkness that stains our world. Evil infiltrates every corner, sometimes in overt and horrifying ways, and other times hidden in the shadows. And if we're not careful, we risk deceiving ourselves into thinking we're immune to such darkness. The reality is, none of us are. Recognizing the power and pervasiveness of evil in our world, and even in our own thoughts, habits, and actions, brings a sense of despair that's hard to shake off.

John 1:5 tells us, "The light shines in the darkness, and the darkness has not overcome it." Within the chaos of sin flooding the world, a firm and hopeful faith endures. Evil is destructive. It seeks to kill, steal, and destroy (John 10:10). It leaves scars on its victims and survivors. Yet, a greater light shines, the Son of God. In the face of darkness, the love of Jesus brings healing, redemption, and the promise of restoration, a hope that can never be extinguished.

Looking again means that we see *all* people as people—and then respond with the decisive and faithful action the moment demands. Seeing people as God does is only the beginning. Standing for what's right isn't just something we choose; as God's image it's what we're called to do.

FOUR WAYS TO KEEP YOUR KIDS SAFE FROM ONLINE ENTICEMENT

1. **GATHER AROUND THE DINNER TABLE EVERY NIGHT:** A face-to-face conversation with your children each night over a meal will help them open up about their day. Creating a space where children can talk about what they are experiencing at school, with their friends, and online offers a way for you to have these serious conversations.

2. **EDUCATE YOUR CHILD ON INTERNET SAFETY:** If you are allowing your children any access to the internet, then a conversation about safety is crucial. By making your children

aware of the dangers online, you can arm them with the tools to navigate potential negative encounters.

3. **ESTABLISH GUARDRAILS FOR TECHNOLOGY USE**: Just like we wouldn't want our children to walk around in public and talk to strangers, we don't want them interacting with people they don't know online. It's important to carry over the rules you establish in the physical world to their online activities. This can include limitations on when and where they use devices and who they talk to. Research apps to help establish digital ground rules.

4. **LEARN THE APPS YOUR CHILDREN ARE USING**: When your children download new apps, make sure you take a few minutes to explore and learn the app yourself. By doing this, you can learn about what safety features you need to turn on while your children are utilizing the app, but you can also take an interest in what they are playing and learning. This can be a way to continue an open dialogue about their online engagement and what interactions they are having with friends.

* Sourced by our ministry partner: National Child Protection Task Force (NCPTF), https://timtebowfoundation.org/stories/four-ways-safeguard-your-kids-predators-online.

Part 3

RUN WITH CONFIDENCE

WE MUST LIVE WITH URGENCY. SOMEONE IS HURTING—NOW. SOMEONE IS CRYING OUT—NOW. SOMEONE IS IN PAIN—NOW. SOMEONE IS BEING HURT, ABUSED, OR EXPLOITED—NOW. AND SOMETHING NEEDS TO BE DONE—NOW.

Chapter 11

A ROYAL RESPONSE

THREE SISTERS—TWIN SIX-YEAR-OLDS AND AN eight-year-old—arrived at one of the safe homes we partner with, barefoot, wearing torn clothes, and infested with lice. Fragile and covered in bruises, they had been physically and sexually abused by their stepfather. Avoiding eye contact, the girls clung to one another, holding hands tightly. Evelyn, a survivor living in the safe house, was there when the sisters arrived. Without hesitation, she offered to help, running upstairs to gather some clothes and all the shoes she owned. Evelyn was left barefoot, but she didn't mind, saying with a smile that the girls needed them more than she did. The staff at the safe house called this sweet girl's actions a miracle, but from anyone looking in, her compassion seemed second nature.

Evelyn had been rescued two years earlier after locals reported suspicions of abuse by her mother. Their concerns sparked a rescue operation that revealed the little girl tied up inside a room. A hurricane had struck, and to keep her daughter from moving, Evelyn's mother had bound her with rope. The restraints etched deep wounds on her wrists, leaving her skin ripped raw from the pressure. One of the little girl's eyes was swollen and black. Lice crawled through the tangled mess of her hair. Dirt caked her fingernails and streaked her skin. But it wasn't Evelyn's appearance that left the deepest mark—it was her haunting cry. For days after her arrival, the five-year-old was inconsolable.

As she began to settle in, Evelyn often told the staff that she didn't know how to love because no one had ever loved her. Years of abuse at her own mother's hands had warped her understanding of the love of God—which she was just beginning to learn about. Yet, over time and with consistent care and counseling, Evelyn's wounds—both seen and unseen—began to heal. Her transformation became evident in the way she instinctively cared for the three sisters who arrived at the safe home. Her actions showed she had not only learned the true meaning of love but had also learned how to share it.

Oftentimes, when we receive love, kindness, mercy, or grace, it naturally inspires us to look again and extend the same to others.

A SACRED RESPONSIBILITY

Theologian J. Richard Middleton has explained that being God's image carries a royal responsibility to represent God. "The *imago Dei* [image of God] designates the royal office or calling of human beings as God's representatives and agents in the world, granted authorized power to share in God's rule or administration of the earth's resources and creatures."[1] As believers in Jesus, reconciled by Him to God, we have a duty to represent our royal heritage as agents of His kingdom.

> As believers in Jesus, reconciled by Him to God, we have a duty to represent our royal heritage as agents of His kingdom.

This sacred responsibility is summed up beautifully in Micah 6:8: "Mankind, he has told each of you what is good and what it is the LORD requires of you: to act justly, to love faithfulness, and to walk humbly with your God" (CSB). Eugene Peterson's paraphrase in *The Message* may paint an even clearer picture: "But [God's] already made it plain how to live, what to do, what GOD is looking for in men and women. It's quite simple: Do what is fair and just to your neighbor, be compassionate and loyal in your love, and don't take yourself too seriously—take God seriously." This is what humanity's original call was in the garden at creation before sin jacked everything up.

The Hebrew word for love in this passage is *hesed*, which is a covenantal, merciful, and redemptive love in action.[2] My favorite definition of the word comes from my dad. He calls *hesed* the greatest form of a loyal love. It doesn't rise and retreat based on our feelings; it shows up in practice. Loving *hesed* means prioritizing the well-being of others and aligning our actions with God's vision for a just world.

That's how we, as His image, reflect God best.

Jesus didn't stop at noticing people; He was moved to act. He taught, shared, comforted, served, and ultimately gave His life. As we are transformed into the likeness of Jesus, we're called to follow His example.

We show mercy as He shows mercy.

Love as He loves.

Forgive as He forgives.

Scripture frequently tells us that Jesus was "moved with compassion." But compassion isn't passive—it's not just pity. It's action. It's being so moved in the deepest part of your spirit that you can't walk away without doing something. Compassion *compels* us to act. Just as Jesus did, we engage with the brokenhearted, the forgotten, and the overlooked. This is love in action. As Paul wrote: "For Christ's love compels us, because we are convinced that one died for all . . . And he died for all, that those who live should no longer live for themselves but for him" (2 Corinthians 5:14–15).

One of my favorite stories from Night to Shine isn't about the lights or the music or the red carpet—it's about a group of volunteers who refused to let anything stand in the way of love.

There was a guest who desperately wanted to come, but he was confined to a specialized medical bed—he couldn't even sit in a wheelchair. The problem? That bed wouldn't fit through the church doors. Most people would have stopped there. They would have said, "It's just not possible." But not this team.

They took the door off the hinges. Then they took off the frame. And when that still wasn't enough—they literally tore down part of the wall. Why? Because one child of God deserved to be celebrated. One person mattered enough to fight for. That's what love looks like. That's what it means to go above and beyond. Night to Shine isn't just about a prom night; it's about showing people they are seen, valued, and worth tearing down walls for. This is the heart of God.

It's easy to say we believe in the worth of every life. It's easy to say we stand against evil. But what do our actions say? Because when it comes to fighting for the dignity and freedom of others, staying on the sidelines isn't neutral; it's a choice. The mindset of "life unworthy of life," that some lives are less valuable than others, has existed throughout history. At its worst, this belief has justified unthinkable atrocities, even under the guise of "compassion." But real compassion isn't about deciding who gets to live and who doesn't. Real compassion means stepping into the fight to protect, defend, and rescue. Every day we ought to ask ourselves: Are we standing for life or watching from a distance? Saying we care while doing nothing?

If actions were a true reflection of beliefs, what story would *ours* tell? Would they say that we believe every person is created in the image of God? That we believe in their worth? Or would our actions, or lack thereof, suggest that we've chosen to look away, that we've left the fight to someone else? What if we actually lived like we believed that every person—every trafficked child, every exploited soul, every abandoned and forgotten life, the ones who don't get invited to the table, and the ones we love the most but we take for granted—was created in the image of God and worthy of freedom?

> Every day we ought to ask ourselves: Are we standing for life or watching from a distance?

Our sacred responsibility to treat others as God's image is far greater than a royal title; it's a life lived for others in practice, not just belief.

A GREAT RESPONSE

Mark 5 records the story of a naked man tormented by a "legion of demons" (v. 15). He was a well-known figure in his community, but not in the way one would like to be. The man was more than a public nuisance. His behavior had become so out of control that the community had resorted to restraining him with chains. It didn't work. So, feeling threatened or unable to understand or respond to his needs (or both), the people saw no other option but to isolate this man from everyone else. He was cast out from the town and forced to live in the tombs. Stripped of all human dignity, the outcast was banished among the dead.

The days and nights blurred into one another. There's not much one can do in the tombs, let alone when possessed by what may have been hundreds of demons. Tormented, while the man drifted between life and death, he scraped jagged rocks across his skin. Blood dripped from the gashes as his cries pierced the air from dusk to dawn.

One day, from a distance, the man saw Jesus approaching by boat across the Sea of Galilee. We don't know how far apart they were—feet, yards, or more—but something about Jesus caught the man's attention. Whether it was a calm presence, an inexplicable sense of divinity, or a few seconds' lock of the eyes, the man saw what he had never seen before in another human being. Immediately, he bolted from the tombs and ran toward Jesus. What happened next shocked the disciples who were with Jesus at the time.

Jesus commanded the demons to leave the man and sent them into a herd of pigs, an animal considered unclean in Jewish culture. The pigs rushed down a bank, plunged into the sea, and drowned. This dramatic display of Jesus' authority served a couple of purposes. It demonstrated His mighty power over demons, news of which reverberated throughout the region. It also freed the possessed man and restored his human dignity.

When it was time for Jesus to return to the other side of the lake, the man who had been healed begged to follow him. Surprisingly, Jesus gave what looked like an uncharacteristic response considering His "follow Me" nature. He said no. Well, *indirectly*. "Go home to your own people," Jesus told the man, "and tell them how much the Lord has done for you, and how he has had mercy on you" (v. 19). Instead of allowing the man to join Him, Jesus told him to return home to the Decapolis—a ten-city region heavily influenced by Greek and Roman culture—and tell his family and neighbors what God had done. The man obeyed and "began to tell in the Decapolis how much Jesus had done for him. And *all the people were amazed*" (v. 20).

This man, once destined to live in the tombs, became one of the first missionaries to non-Jewish communities, spreading the news of

Jesus' compassion and authority. God's mission for him was different from what he had envisioned, but it was a response worthy of the healing and restoration he had received.

One of my pastor friends likes to say, "Every good gift demands a great response." It's a powerful line. But even more, it's a powerful way to live. Just like the man in Mark 5, believers have been given the extraordinary gifts of inheriting eternal life and the fullness of God's kingdom and being empowered by the Holy Spirit to live out our royal identity. These gifts demand a *great* response.

A *GET* TO, NOT A *HAVE* TO

What if we truly grasped not just the responsibility but also the great honor and privilege of responding to the greatest gift ever given—Jesus? Let that sink in.

God didn't have to give us this responsibility. He could have trusted angels or other celestial beings to proclaim His message. He could have used carrier pigeons, snow-capped mountains, the roar of a raging sea, or the whisper of the wind to share the gospel. But instead, He entrusted us with it. He handed the greatest message of all time— the only message that saves, reconciles, delivers, heals, and renews all things—into our hands and said, "Go into all the world and preach the gospel to all creation" (Mark 16:15).

Tell them they can be saved. Tell them they can have hope. Tell them they can be free. Tell them they are loved no matter what. Tell them they can live with Me forever in paradise.

Let's pause and revisit *euangelion*, the Greek word for gospel I mentioned in chapter 6, meaning "good news."[3] In ancient Greco-Roman times, *euangelion* didn't mean your average good news ("The band is back together!" or "My favorite kicks are on sale!"). Announcing a military victory or the rise of a new king also wasn't just personal news but a message that was meant for everyone. The gospel is an invitation for all people to participate in God's kingdom come, not just a select few. What an honor that is! It's why my dad can't help but tear up whenever he talks or hear about the good news. Even in his seventies and having known Christ since early in his college days, my dad's heart is still tender to the message of hope, a quality I pray I can emulate.

It's all about perspective. It's easy to settle into the mindset of sharing the good news, in words and action, as a chore or obligation. I *have* to do this. We view telling others of hope as an obligation rather than an opportunity. But that type of mindset is misguided, and sometimes we need to look again.

It's not "I *have* to"—it's "I *get* to."

Just like in sports, there's a difference between the player who groans, *"Ugh, I have to go to practice"* and the one who says, *"I get to go to practice today."* The difference? Love. Somewhere along the way, even if we don't lose the love for God, we lose the love of the message. We forget what a privilege it is to share the hope of Jesus. To stand before a world that's desperate and lonely and burdened and say, "Let me show you the way to life, a life that's different and better than even what your greatest imagination can conceive." When we grasp this power in our own lives, how can we keep quiet about the power of God to save, heal, redeem, and rescue? Someone cared enough to share this message with us; how can we not forward this great hope?

The way we carry out sharing the gospel will look different for each of us. The method doesn't matter as much as the mindset. It may come from standing on a stage, handing someone a tract or a Bible, praying with or having a one-on-one conversation with a friend or a stranger. One thing is certain, being plugged into this mindset will move the needle from a life lived for ourselves to one that's focused on others.

Ethan, one of our W15H kids I've written about in my book *Mission Possible*, is the embodiment of a great response. Despite being diagnosed with stage 4 neuroblastoma at nine years old, he was a testament to the power of God to work in one's life despite pain, sickness, and weakness. If he was given an opportunity to share his faith, for example, Ethan never let it slip by.

A NOT-SO-CHANCE ENCOUNTER

On June 30, 2010, Ethan Hallmark was diagnosed with stage 4 neuroblastoma and began the fight of his life. He was nine years old. I met him, his parents, and his grandfather on September 20, 2012, during a W15H event, a one-on-one personalized experience our foundation creates for children with life-threatening illnesses. At the time, I was playing with the New York Jets at an away game in Pittsburgh. Ethan left an incredible mark on me—and everyone he met—because of his kind spirit and deep love for Jesus. Before the game, he asked if he could pray for me. (Yes, the kid with a life-threatening illness was the one praying for the healthy adult football player! That's the kind of young man he was!) His faith was unshakable. After the game, Ethan and I talked in the locker room for so long that I ended up late for the bus ride to our next destination. Being around him made you want to hold on to every moment.

Two years after I met him, when Ethan was thirteen years old, on palliative care actively dying, he was asked to be in the *I Am Second* series, a collection of short documentary-style videos, which feature personal stories of people whose lives have been transformed through faith. Rachel, his mother, remembers preparing her son for filming by writing a script for him to remember the most impactful memories of his life. Ethan respectfully brushed his mom off, assuring her he knew what had happened in his own life. Right after filming wrapped up, Ethan remembered something he forgot to share. "Wait," he told the crew, "I want to share my favorite Bible verse." And as the cameras rolled for the last time, Ethan recited Psalm 40:5: "Many, Lord my God, are the wonders you have done, the things you planned for us. None can compare with you."

Think about the magnitude of that moment. Here was a thirteen-year-old boy who had been told that nothing more could be done by doctors or treatments, a boy living what he knew would be the final weeks of his life. And out of all the things he could have shared, he chose a scripture that highlighted the incredible wonders of God! This speaks volumes about Ethan and his faith—far better than I ever could.

No matter how much pain he was in, how tired he was, or the depth of his discouragement when facing unexpected news that the cancer had spread, Ethan lived on purpose. He wrote, "Cancer may knock me down at times, but God is the ultimate builder. None of us know what the future holds, but in all things we know God has special plans for every one of us. If we have faith, we have eternity with our Heavenly Father. It is always a win/win situation for those who believe in God."[4] Ethan never hesitated to respond to others about his faith, no matter the time or place.

In November 2011, thanks to a sponsored trip by the Make-A-Wish foundation, Ethan and his family were in Hawaii so Ethan could enjoy one of his passions, fishing. One morning, as the sun lit up the Maui horizon, Ethan and his mom stood barefoot on the sandy shore, enjoying a simple moment fishing.

At the same time, a man in his twenties named Aaron Palmer sat nearby on the beach. Hungover from the night before, a vodka bottle tucked into his back pocket hinted at the bender he was on. Aaron had been a raging alcoholic, blacking out multiple times a week, for years. Then came the DUI, requiring a night stay in jail. Right after Aaron was released, he walked into a bar. The addiction cycle continued. Two months after getting arrested, he went to Maui to celebrate a friend's wedding. His trip was fuzzy, having blacked out from drinking every day. One morning, having promised himself he wouldn't return home without watching a Hawaiian sunrise, Aaron dragged his hungover self to the beach. It was then he noticed a little boy fishing with what looked to be his mother. Armed with liquid courage, Aaron felt compelled to walk over and speak to the two strangers on the beach. Rachel explained to Aaron her son's battle with cancer. And for reasons he will never understand, she allowed him to talk to her son after asking her permission.

Aaron and Ethan talked for about thirty minutes. Though Aaron doesn't remember the particulars, he will never forget the effect it had on him. "I saw a boy facing death who had more faith, and more happiness, and more hope than I had in my entire life."[5] Walking back to his hotel room after the conversation, Aaron thought long and hard about his life. "How can I continue, knowing this boy is happier than me and has so much faith?" Aaron left Hawaii and went back home a transformed man. He got sober and found God. He shared, "With sobriety, my faith grew. I leaned in. I talked to God. I realized that He's my friend. He loves me, I'm His son."[6]

Twelve years after getting sober, in 2023, Aaron was encouraged to find "the boy on the beach" since he never remembered Ethan's name. He googled and emailed a bunch of different departments and people at Make-A-Wish. No responses seemed promising. One day, the CEO of Make-A-Wish North Texas called and said, "Aaron, we found him. His parents want to talk to you."[7]

For the first time, Aaron had a name to the boy he met on the beach: Ethan. One day around Christmas, Ethan's family and Aaron finally met. Aaron had the opportunity to tell Rachel; her husband, Matt; and their children how much Ethan had changed his life. He showed them pictures of his own kids—children who have a father today because of Ethan. The day on the beach wasn't random. It was a divine moment that sparked healing, growth, and a new purpose in the life of a man who was drinking himself to death.[8] Aaron said, "There's a ripple effect that's flowing through my family because of Ethan. And it's just not done."[9]

Though Ethan and Aaron connected only for a few minutes one day, they share something special. Ethan died on September 26, 2014. September 26 also happens to be Aaron's birthday. It was more than just a chance encounter.

Ethan and his mom had every reason to savor the peace, quiet, and beauty of a Maui sunrise without interruption. After all, this was his actual wish, a trip to Hawaii planned just for him so he could enjoy one of his passions. Ethan could have been too tired, had too much pain, or not been in the mood to chat with a random guy on the beach. Rachel could have dismissed the stranger's approach, uncomfortable and leery of his intentions. She might have craved a rare moment alone with her son, away from the endless grind of hospitals and treatments. But Ethan and his mom didn't turn away. They understood what it means to be God's image on a journey marked by calamity. And they showed up—not with grand gestures or profound words that may not have been remembered, but with simple obedience. And, in doing so, they reflected God's love in a way that spoke louder than anything they could have said.

WHY WOULDN'T WE RESPOND?

We say we believe the gospel, but if that's true—why wouldn't we live it? As believers we have the privilege not just to believe in Jesus but to become the gospel, to step into the mission of God as both recipients and agents of grace. More than a truth we accept, it's a calling we embody.

So, why do we respond? Out of a love for Jesus, for people, for the vulnerable and the broken? Out of gratitude for what God has done for us? Out of marvel at our own transformation and desiring the same for others? Do we respond out of urgency because this is the only message that saves? Yes—to all the above.

Again, living for Jesus is not a me thing; it's a we thing. When we say yes to the gospel, we don't just get to receive it, we get to carry it, to be agents of change in a broken world.

The real question isn't *Why should we respond?* The real question is *Why wouldn't we?*

Chapter 12

LIVES ON THE LINE

GUNTHER WAS BORN IN 1914 IN GERMANY WITH severe physical deformities. Over the years, his mind and body deteriorated due to malnutrition. Unable to walk or use his hands, he spent most of his days confined to his bed in a back room of his grandmother's house. Frustrated by Gunther's lack of capacity to do anything, she constantly referred to the boy as "no good for anything" and "human junk."[1] When he was six years old, Gunther's grandmother dropped him off at Bethel, an institution that cared for children and adults with special needs, where he would remain for the rest of his life.

Edna Hong, renowned for translating Soren Kierkegaard's works into English, wrote a book about Gunther. She described an awakening the little boy had at Bethel. Hearing new stories about Jesus and God's love, Gunther experienced what Hong called "a dim and jumbled but wildly wonderful realization of the possibility of life— that he was not a piece of human garbage carried along on a gray and endless tide of time."[2] For the first time, thanks to the people who cared at Bethel, Gunther realized he was a beloved child of the King of the universe.

While Gunther lived at Bethel, the institution was led by Friedrich von Bodelschwingh, a pastor in the Confessing Church during the 1930s, where Dietrich Bonhoeffer influenced its spiritual foundation. When Gunther was around twenty-six years old, T4, the euthanasia program mentioned in the first chapter, was being rolled out.[3] The Nazi government, as it had done with other institutions, demanded that Bethel provide a list of "incurables," individuals with disabilities marked for euthanasia.[4] Individuals like Gunther.

Acknowledging the worth of people who much of society shunned and believing that to serve the vulnerable was a privilege, von Bodelschwingh refused.[5] He continued to fight for the vulnerable under his care by communicating his opposition to the government. Von Bodelschwingh wasn't alone in his stance. There are records of others, both clergy and medical professionals, who resisted the Nazi regime's persecution of individuals with disabilities.

In 1939, Dr. Walter Creutz, a medical officer in the German army, began to hear rumors of T4. When he was reassigned to a post in western Germany as the head of the Rhine province's mental hospital system, he learned the gossip was true and tried to come up with a plan to push back against the program. In 1941, Dr. Creutz persuaded the governor of the Rhineland to resist the order, but when a state official handed the governor Hitler's directive in person, the governor swiftly reversed course and withdrew all objections to the killing of people with disabilities.

At this point, Dr. Creutz oversaw the transit centers that temporarily housed victims to be transported to the killing centers. He chose to stay in his position, believing it was better to try to quietly sabotage the program from within rather than leave and be replaced by a non-sympathetic member of the Nazi Party. Talk about a moral dilemma. Stand up for what's right and risk losing your influence for change—or worse, your life—or choose compliance and attempt to have impact in the shadows? No easy answer here.

Locking arms with other heads of mental institutions and nursing homes, he proposed broadening the criteria for exemptions, such as reclassifying schizophrenia in elderly patients as age-related cognitive decline and thus prevent them from being transferred to a killing center. He even coached some families on how to petition for their family member to be released from the transit center. Though hundreds of patients were sent off to be killed beyond their control, he and other medical professionals were able to mitigate some impact. Court records revealed that out of 5,046 patients slated for transfer to a killing center, approximately 4,100 were successfully spared from transport.

Other German physicians did similar things, including Dr. Karl Todt and Dr. Adolf Thiel, who oversaw another transit center. They sabotaged T4 by discharging patients, overstating patients' ability to work and their value to the institution, and hiding severely disabled patients when officials of the T4 commission would visit. Court records show that these doctors saved 20 percent of their patients from being murdered.[6]

Germans outside the medical community also took a stand against the euthanasia program. Clemens August Graf von Galen, a bishop in the Roman Catholic Church who would later become a cardinal, gave several sermons from behind a pulpit protesting the killing of people with disabilities. In one message about the inherent worth of all human life, von Galen said, "If you establish and apply the principle that you can kill 'unproductive' fellow human beings then woe betide us all when we become old and frail! . . . It is only necessary for some secret edict to order that the method developed for the mentally ill should be extended to other 'unproductive' people."[7]

Germany is often vilified for the atrocities committed by the Nazis against the Jewish people and other vulnerable groups. Yet, as you've seen throughout this book, the marginalization of the vulnerable is a global issue, including in the country where I live. Disability rights activist Hugh Gallagher noted that "the Germans are not 'different' from Americans in any critical sense." Gallagher went on to note that how they treated those with a disability "during the Third Reich was certainly extreme behavior—tragic and appalling—but it was not inconsistent with patterns of social behavior that can be traced throughout the history of the disabled over the centuries."[8]

Gallagher was right. The vulnerable have been disparaged throughout ancient and modern civilizations. Whether viewing those with disabilities as a curse from the gods, or killing babies who were "not adequate," or emphasizing hierarchy by ostracizing the poor,[9] history evidences the marginalization of the vulnerable as well as their inclusive care by individuals who advocated for the inherent worth of all human beings. The bottom line is that despite progress, vulnerable groups continue to endure challenges, from systemic inequality to stigma, abuse, and exploitation.

We've all got work to do. And while some people may criticize what Germans like Friedrich von Bodelschwingh and Dr. Creutz did as a passive move of resistance against the Nazis' targeting of people with special needs, they still responded. And in whatever way they were able to, they rescued image *beings*.

A SENSE OF URGENCY

One of my favorite ways to talk about the birth, life, death, and resurrection of Jesus is as a *rescue mission*. Once we put our faith in Him, we have been rescued. But after we've been rescued, the mission isn't over. Like one of our pastors and close friends Joby Martin always says, "We're now on the *rescue team*." That means we're invited to partner with God to show and share His love with a world that desperately needs it. Would anyone in your life say that you live like you're on a rescue team?

> Would anyone in your life say that you live like you're on a rescue team?

Do the gospel and hurting people compel you enough to live with such urgency, focus, and sacrifice as if you were on a rescue team? It's a convicting concept, isn't it? Moms, you know this better than anyone—you're on a rescue mission every day, loving, guiding, and fighting for your kids! Living like you're on a rescue team necessitates more than most are willing to give. It's not always easy. But having this mentality matters. Why? Because people's lives are at stake.

When's the last time you heard of a rescue team planning out a rescue mission taking place five years from now? That's right, probably never! Why? Because there's a sense of urgency in the word *rescue*. A rescue team doesn't sit on their heels and wait for the dust to settle. Of course, strategy is involved, but action is also taken, and quickly.

One of the reasons my dad is my greatest hero is because he's quick to act. One of my favorite stories of Dad is from his time as a missionary in Southeast Asia. A young girl, whose mother died at childbirth and whose father had abandoned the family, was about to be thrown into a river by her grandpa. Whether out of desperation or ill-intent, that was her fate. However, when my dad heard about this, he sent an urgent message to one of his team members who was close by the river. Without hesitation, this team member was able to rescue the little girl. Nicknamed "Queenie" by Dad because he wanted her to know that she was a *queen* in God's eyes, this little girl inspired him to establish an orphanage.

What I love about this story is that my dad didn't hesitate! He could have ignored the news, dismissed it because he didn't know the girl personally or because he wasn't there. But he didn't. Dad acted with urgency. Not for a pat on the back or for applause. But for the sake of the gospel and for the sake of people.

In my TV room sits an hourglass gifted to me by a friend after writing my last book. Bolted to a slim wooden base, a ceramic bronze hand stands tall with its palm up and its fingers outstretched, cradling the hourglass itself. With a magnet on both ends, the hourglass fits perfectly in the hand, a symbol of God holding time in His hand. Etched into the base is a quote from one of my favorite people you just read about, Ethan: *"It doesn't matter whether you live to 1 or 100, what matters is what you do for Christ."* As the white sand falls from one end to the other, I'm reminded that the clock is ticking. Time is running out. What matters is what we do for Christ.

> Time is running out. What matters is what we do for Christ.

We must live with urgency. Someone is hurting—now. Someone is crying out—now. Someone is in pain—now. Someone is being hurt, abused, or exploited—now. And something needs to be done—now.

Let me be clear. None of us hold the power to defeat evil; that's God's job. And while on this side of heaven it's not going to happen completely, we have been empowered to snatch as many people from darkness as we can. If that's not a rescue mission that requires our immediate intervention, I don't know what is.

This great need offers us an opportunity to do something, to fight for those who can't fight for themselves. I know you care—or at least

I hope you do. When we see God's image hurting, do we care *enough* to do something?

APATHY, ACTION'S ARCHNEMESIS

There's no doubt that many of us are moved to some degree when we're confronted with darkness. At the same time, many of us are so overwhelmed by it that we become paralyzed. We stay silent. We do nothing. Enter apathy.

Professor and theologian Uche Anizor defined apathy as a "psychological and spiritual sickness in which we experience a prolonged dampening of motivation, effort, and emotion."[10] Another way he put it, apathy is "not the hostility of a shaking fist but of a gaping yawn."[11] For a word that has much to do with nothingness, the cost of apathy is astronomical.

Why do many of us flirt with or indulge apathy and risk doing nothing? The answers lie in the questions we ask ourselves:

Where do I even start?

Can someone like me really make a difference?

How can I care for others when I'm already overwhelmed by my own struggles?

How do I choose which cause or need to focus on when they all seem urgent?

Why would anyone need my help? People who are more capable ought to be running the show!

None of these questions suggest a lack of care or concern. And it's certainly not a sin to ask them. For many of us, however, these questions alone become precursors for doing nothing. Yes, it's easy to feel overwhelmed by the scale of suffering in the world or even by the struggles in our own microcosms. And because we're constantly exposed to negative news, it's not so hard to become desensitized to the pain around us.

Whether apathy stems from disillusionment with broken systems, compassion fatigue, a sense of powerlessness, or even an outright desire to avoid responsibility and hard things, one outcome is certain if we let it linger: Nothing changes, and often, things only get worse.

One thing that's helped to snap me out of the temptation to do nothing is remembering what Christ has done for me. I've gone from old to new, slave to free, dead to alive! Our true power lies beyond the limits of our flesh and blood. As God's image, we are empowered by a source that is eternal, incorruptible, and everlasting.

> As God's image, we are empowered by a source that is eternal, incorruptible, and everlasting.

In a scene in *Batman Begins*, the first movie in *The Dark Knight* trilogy, Bruce Wayne has just returned home from traveling the world to gain an understanding of the criminal underworld. Upon reuniting with his butler, Alfred, Bruce explains his plans to return to Gotham City to fight crime, not as himself but as Batman. Alfred reminds Bruce how Bruce's father almost bankrupted his company to help the poor, hoping his example would serve as a catalyst to inspire fellow successful people of Gotham to save their city.

Bruce: "Did it?"

Alfred: "In a way. Their murders shocked the wealthy and the powerful into action."

Bruce's response hit me hard: "People need dramatic examples to shake them out of apathy, and I can't do that as Bruce Wayne. As a man, I'm flesh and blood. I can be ignored. I can be destroyed. But as a symbol, I can be incorruptible, I can be everlasting."[12]

While putting on a mask and becoming a caped crusader is

something that happens only in the movies, as believers we can respond. Yes, we can leap tall buildings in a single bound, figuratively of course, not because we're superheroes but because King Jesus, better than a caped crusader, invites us to be on His team. We can love. We can forgive. We can show mercy. We can listen. We can shake ourselves and others out of the dullness of apathy and care enough to join the rescue mission. Jesus was a dramatic example in His day, and you can be too. The image in you is an everlasting symbol—a symbol that must show the world the dramatic, scandalous, inconceivable *love* of God.

My antidote to apathy? The regret of missed opportunities, the times I could have acted but didn't. I don't want to live with that kind of regret. I want to honor God, to say yes to Him, and to love what He loves most—people. The reality that God loves me and that He loves others is the driving force in my heart and mind, pushing me to live a life of meaning, not indifference. Because when you see people hurting, when you think about the timeline of your life and the urgency of the need, waiting isn't an option. Patience has its place, but not when lives are hanging in the balance.

The call is clear—God's Word is clear. We're called to love, to care for, and to defend the hurting. We may not understand everything, but will we say yes? Will we act in the face of uncertainty, trusting that God will lead us? Or will we sit back, waiting for everything to make sense? Sometimes all we need to do is take the first step and say yes, knowing that as we keep moving, He'll show us the rest.

THROUGH THE ROOF

The Bible records the story of the paralytic in Luke 5, Matthew 9, and Mark 2. Let's look at it in Luke:

One day Jesus was teaching, and Pharisees and teachers of the law were sitting there. They had come from every village of Galilee and from Judea and Jerusalem. And the power of the Lord was with Jesus to heal the sick. Some men came carrying a paralyzed man on a mat and tried to take him into the house to lay him before Jesus. When they could not find a way to do this because of the crowd, they went up on the roof and lowered him on his mat through the tiles into the middle of the crowd, right in front of Jesus. When Jesus saw their faith, he said, "Friend, your sins are forgiven." (Luke 5:17–20)

A few observations about this story: We're not told how the man became paralyzed. It could have been from an accident, a disease, or a condition he'd had since birth. We also don't know the relationship of the men to the one they carried on the mat. Here's what we do know.

We know that Luke's Gospel uniquely emphasizes the word *front* as in "in *front* of Jesus" two times (vv. 19, 25). These men were convinced that something would happen, something life-changing, if they got this man in *front* of Jesus. So, they did something dramatic. They climbed to the roof of the house in which Jesus was speaking and destroyed it (well, likely just a portion of it). Mark 2:4 tells us the men dug through the roof. Roofs in those days were made by placing branches over the ceiling beams and packing them with mud. The roof would have been strong enough to support the men walking on it but soft enough to put a hole through it without needing a power tool.

Picture the chaotic scene. The gasps of shock as a cloud of dust and dirt rained down from the ceiling, followed by chunks of hardened mud and broken branches. The sudden beam of light shooting through a gaping hole in the roof. The man on the mat, slowly descending, inch by inch toward the stunned crowd.

Desperate times call for drastic measures.

In this biblical account, the healing of the paralyzed man often gets the spotlight, but his four friends—the ones who broke through the roof—have rightfully earned attention too. These men were hopeful that Jesus could help their friend, but getting him into the right place for that to happen wasn't going to be easy. I imagine they explored other options before settling on their bold, through-the-roof strategy. They must have brainstormed and planned. You know what that tells me? They recognized an urgent need, cared enough, and acted. They didn't tear down the doors; they tore down the roof. What a great example for us to follow.

When's the last time you went out of your way to put someone before Jesus? When's the last time you broke through a roof because you knew the urgency of a need? When's the last time you were so compelled to act, you surrendered your agenda and threw apathy out the window?

When's the last time you cared *enough* to do something?

At our foundation, I remind everyone that we are fighting for what holds the greatest eternal value: people. Whether or not we're on the front lines of rescue missions, every role matters. From fundraising to accounting to scheduling, every action creates a ripple effect that drives the mission forward. It's easy to lose sight of this when we're not directly engaged with those we're helping, making it tempting to go through the motions and let apathy creep in. But even without face-to-face contact, every effort we make to move the needle forward carries immense impact. Knowing this fuels a relentless sense of urgency in our hearts and minds, which inevitably leads to action.

There's no one-size-fits-all blueprint for a rescue mission; each one is unique. Take Ethan and Aaron's interaction, for example. It was a rescue mission in its own way, even though none of them realized it at the time. Despite the many moving parts, every rescue mission shares a common foundation: the unwavering belief that every life has value and transformation is possible. At its core, every rescue mission is fueled by hope.

BEING A HOPE CARRIER

Recently, I was in the Philippines, the country where I was born and one I love very much. We're fortunate to have established a hospital in Davao City in Mindanao, the second-largest island in the Philippines, where we have the opportunity to treat and care for kids all over the country who are born with disabilities like clubfoot and cleft lip and palate. We also provide physical therapy, medical devices like wheelchairs, and biblical counseling.

A few years ago, we were celebrating NTS at several locations throughout the Philippines. We also spent time visiting the patients and staff at our hospital. Toward the end of that day, because our group was large in number, we split up for the remaining two visits to check in with and love on those we'd served at the hospital. Demi led one team to one house, and I led the other to the home of a young teenage girl who had undergone multiple surgeries.

The first girl we visited came from a family of more than five people, all living together in a two-room house smaller than the bedroom Demi and I share. The dirt floor kicked up dust with every step. Thin mattresses were scattered on the ground. Children peeked behind curtains that separated rooms. Clothes hung drying from a wire strung across the walls.

Our team spent time talking with the girl and her parents, then prayed with them. As we thanked the family for their kind hospitality and left for the next visit, my heart felt both heavy and hopeful.

There's something about desperation that breaks a language barrier. The boy's uncle didn't need perfect words to tell me he felt desperate. I sensed this man was starving for something: hope. But not hope for just himself. Hope for his nephew. Maybe I could help by pointing them to our team so they could be a hope carrier.

That encounter reminded me of the responsibility and privilege we have to bring hope to those around us—wherever we are. None of us need to travel halfway around the world to find people who are desperate and starving for hope. They exist all around us: in our schools, our communities, even in our churches.

The way I often hear the word *hope* used seems flippant. *I hope my favorite team wins. I hope I get the job. I hope she likes me.* Hope in this sense holds as much weight as flipping a coin and seeing where it lands. Giving true hope to people isn't about being driven by feelings, because frankly, emotions are fickle and can change—and fast—based on external situations. Trust me, I know. One of my greatest struggles is managing my emotions; they can swing from high to low, sometimes in the same moment.

The best biblical definition for hope is to look forward with confidence, expectation, and anticipation. That form of hope isn't based on a wish or a coin flip but on biblical promises that are kept.

Why can we look forward with confidence? Because we win!

Why can we look forward with expectation? Because God's got a great plan for us!

Why can we look forward with anticipation? Because our best days—heaven—are ahead of us!

> The best biblical definition for hope is to look forward with confidence, expectation, and anticipation.

Imagine if we used the word *hope* not as a passing fancy but a way of life. Imagine if everywhere we went—at home, at the office, on the field—we created a culture of biblical hope that looks forward with confidence, expectation, and anticipation. As God's image, this is one way we can represent Him and take responsibility to help others who are also made as His image. Our response to a world that lacks hope, to the growing loneliness and mental illness epidemic? It lies within you and me. It lies within everyone who represents God as His image.

Even though evil is at work in the world, we have a hope that is grounded in God's promises, not in our own strength or actions. When we look at the magnitude of darkness, it's easy to feel overwhelmed, but the key is to stop comparing the size of the problem to ourselves. When we compare it to the size of our God, we remember there is no match. Like David faced Goliath, we need to stand firm in the fact that no evil can stand against the power of our God.

Our role in all this is to keep saying yes. Yes to Jesus. Yes to people. Yes to the mission. Yes to the small or big steps He asks us to take. We might not see the full picture, and we certainly don't know how God will use our yes, but we can trust that His plan is sufficient and that it is *always* worth it.

RETHINKING STEWARDSHIP

I'm often asked, "Isn't there a risk when we use what we have to bring hope to others?" A risk in this sense might be anything from social rejection, emotional vulnerability, financial loss, personal sacrifices, even physical danger. I can't help but wonder: Is it truly a gamble when we leverage what we have for eternity, for God's purposes? When we acknowledge that everything we have isn't ours to begin with but His, the narrative shifts.

Stewardship is often thought of only in terms of money, time, and resources. But the Bible teaches that stewardship is a far greater concept. It is our response to the gifts God has given us; stewardship is how we live our life. In the New Testament, the Greek word for stewardship, *oikonomos*, refers to someone entrusted with the management of a household or property—a caretaker, not an owner.[13] In the parables of Jesus, stewards are often depicted as individuals who are responsible for managing the resources of their master, with the *expectation* that they will do so wisely and faithfully (Luke 12:42–48; Matthew 25:14–30). This role was not merely about managing finances but involved a broader sense of responsibility. In other words, like royals, we are tasked with managing what God has placed in our hands for His purposes.

I think about a friend of mine—a true hero. He's served our country with extraordinary courage, enduring countless injuries on the battlefield. He's been blown up, put back together, and, even after all that, continued serving the world's most vulnerable. Recently, he was injured again while protecting others, and now he's fighting to save his leg. Not long ago, I FaceTimed him. I told him how incredibly grateful I am for his sacrifice.

"Man, I'm so sorry for this," I said. "Thank you for everything you've done—for putting yourself on the line for so many people. I'm so sorry about your leg."

He responded with words that stopped me in my tracks: "Thank you, but honestly, it's not even mine anyway." He was talking about his leg. Wow! That's what stewardship looks like. It's the recognition that everything—our time, our resources, even our very bodies—is not ours to hold on to but rather to give for the sake of others and the glory of God.[14]

When my friend and I ended the call, I had to walk onto a stage to speak, but I couldn't find the words. I was overwhelmed by his example of sacrificial stewardship.

Biblical stewardship has to do with understanding that your life is not your own. Your life is on loan from God, whether you acknowledge this or not. And from Jesus' parable of the talents (Matthew 25:14–30), it seems clear that as believers we're called to leverage and steward everything about our lives for His glory and the good of others. Whether it's finances, relationships, time, or even our physical well-being, we are called to steward it well, knowing that it's all His.

We are invited to join the greatest rescue mission in history, one that's made possible by Jesus' sacrifice on the cross. He has entrusted us with the mission of bringing hope to a world in desperate need. Ignoring darkness because it's too disturbing shouldn't be an option. While thoughts and prayers are game changers, rescue missions demand our proximity and engagement. The need is urgent. We're not operating on our own timeline but on the timelines of those crying out for help. Take another look, and then put love into action.

> We are invited to join the greatest rescue mission in history, one that's made possible by Jesus' sacrifice on the cross.

Chapter 13

ANOTHER LOOK

A FEW WEEKS BEFORE SUBMITTING THIS MANU-script, I found myself surrounded by boxes of trophies, jerseys, cleats, fragments of a life I had dreamed would play out a certain way. These memorabilia had been sitting in my TV room for years, collecting dust and waiting for me to decide what to do with them. A friend had come over to help. As we unpacked each item, my eyes dampened, reliving memories as I held my College Hall of Fame jersey, a uniform from high school, photographs from SEC championships, the eye black I wore with John 3:16, and more. I smiled at photos from teammates and friends and rode an emotional wave remembering the highs and lows of playing sports. A little more than three years earlier, I had been cut from the Jacksonville Jaguars. Perspective can be the easiest thing to lose and the hardest thing to gain. Each box I pried open brought back disappointment of unanswered questions from that time: *Is this the moment that defines all my years of grinding, my last shot at sports? Is this what people will remember most about me?*

When the last box stood bare, peace settled in my spirit. It felt like God was reminding me that He had traded what in my eyes looked like a failed plan for what was in His eyes a greater purpose. I told you what it felt like when I was cut from the Jags, but I didn't share what happened immediately after. That moment didn't end in disappointment; it became a launching point for something even greater.

In 2021, after nearly two decades of having boots on the ground, the United States withdrew its troops from Afghanistan, bringing an end to its military presence there. But that moment also left behind a nation and many people in crisis. Several critical and tragic events unfolded before that day, including a suicide bombing in the Kabul airport that killed 13 US service members and 170 Afghan civilians. As our foundation watched the tragedy unfold and heard firsthand accounts from our partners and friends on the ground, we felt an increasing responsibility to step in and help in any way we could.

During this crisis, I had the opportunity to fly to the Middle East and witness the chaos firsthand, to stand among those who were fighting for their lives. This all unfolded around the same time I got cut from the Jaguars. I was still raw. Mad at God and disappointed in myself. After spending time ministering in one country, I flew to a second. Somewhere on that flight, something shifted in me. Meeting brave soldiers and refugee families helped me to look again. And for the first time, I thanked God for getting cut. What felt like a setback was actually a setup. If I had made the team, I never would have been available to step into that moment—to serve, to love, to fight for those who can't fight for themselves. That's just like God. He sees the whole picture.

Looks can be deceiving. They don't always tell the whole story. Think of Jesus on the cross, bloodied, battered, and seemingly defeated. To those watching, it didn't look like a picture of hope, but of despair. But God saw beyond that moment. He knew the cross wasn't the end of the story but the gateway to resurrection and eternal life.

What looked like loss was actually victory! That's the power of looking again, seeing beyond the surface to what God sees.

In the same way, value isn't always obvious at first glance. Take a red carpet—more than just fabric, to most of us it carries meaning, prestige, and a sense of purpose. But what is it that makes it so valuable?

YOU CAN'T ROLL UP WORTH

For centuries, the red carpet has symbolized prestige and exclusivity, its history woven through myth, high society, and Hollywood glamour. First referenced in the Greek tragedy *Agamemnon* (458 BCE), it was deemed fit only for gods.[1] By the nineteenth century, it was in elite events and later marked luxury train travel. According to one historian, the red carpet "symbolized status, something most people had no access to."[2]

Hollywood embraced the tradition in 1922, rolling it out for *Robin Hood*, forever linking the red carpet with stardom. By 1961, televised coverage cemented its role as the stage for entertainment's elite, where fashion, fame, and aspiration collide at events like the Grammys, Academy Awards, and the Oscars. When it comes to the Oscars, there's one little-known mystery: What happens to the red carpet? Weighing up to 630 pounds and requiring nine hundred hours to install, no one knows where it goes when the award show is over, other than it's not used again.[3]

As I mentioned before, every Night to Shine is a little different, depending on location, culture, and weather, but there is one thing that every NTS event must have: a red carpet. Each honored guest we serve is invited to walk, roll, or be carried on this strip of bold fabric when they arrive. The carpet is lined with volunteer paparazzi who celebrate MVP kings and queens as they make their way down. It's one of the ways we show our guests they are important. They are extravagantly loved and intricately designed. They matter so much that Jesus gave His life for them. They are royalty.

The history of people with disabilities reveals the sobering truth that throughout history they have been met with fear, prejudice, and intolerance, often subjected to "infanticide, starved, burned, shunned and isolated, strangled, submerged in hot water, beaten, chained and caged, tortured, gassed, shot, sterilized, warehoused and sedated, hanged, and used as amusement."[4] Though society's treatment, even today, may not value people with special needs, at NTS they belong on the red carpet.

Recently at the end of an NTS in Guatemala, as people were beginning to clean up glasses of water, juice, and punch; deflate balloons; and collect the leftover fidget toys and neon sunglasses our guests love, I noticed some of our volunteers wrapping up the last task. I couldn't stop staring as they rolled up the red carpet to be cleaned, stored, and reused the next year. When they laid it to the side, I started thinking that at first glance this long piece of scarlet fabric is just carpet. There's nothing inherently valuable or special about it. Sure, the red carpet at the Oscars costs close to $25,000, but it's easy to find one for under a hundred bucks.[5] It's not the value of a red carpet that matters at NTS but the message it carries that holds importance. It speaks to the worth of the individuals who find themselves on it. Alongside the cheering volunteers, most of whom leave with hoarse voices at the end of the night—the red carpet shouts to our honored guests:

"God sees you!"

"You are special!"

"You are royalty!"

At the end of the night, the red carpet is removed from the swath of grass, hotel hallway, or the front entrance of a church where it was laid, as if it was never there, but the message behind it stays the same. You can roll up a piece of fabric, but you can't roll away the inherent worth and value of every individual who was celebrated on it—or any human being that has ever been born.

In God's economy, every day is red carpet season.

> In God's economy, every day is red carpet season.

CHOCOLATE CAKE

John is nonverbal and has both autism and Down syndrome. In his mom Abigail's words, "It's an unusual combination that makes everyday life unpredictable and challenging." Simple outings like going to the mall or attending a family barbecue often turn into carefully orchestrated efforts to minimize John's discomfort and manage his outbursts. Walking into a room means being prepared for anything, including tantrums that can easily last for hours.

Getting John fitted for a tuxedo for his first NTS brought out doubt in Abigail. He screamed and cried the entire time. His reaction was so disturbing, Abigail began to doubt whether attending NTS made sense or would prove to be just as difficult. John went anyway.

The process of getting John ready and out the door for the celebration proved chaotic. Furious because his dinner time was interrupted, he howled and protested every step of the way, from getting into the car to getting out and onto the red carpet. When John burst into a full-blown temper tantrum on the red carpet, Abigail began to weep. But it wasn't because she was frustrated with John's behavior. Her tears flowed because for the first time, she watched her son be celebrated.

As volunteer paparazzi cheered and encouraged him and the other guests, she could hardly believe that her child—the one so often gawked at, met with dirty looks, or ignored entirely—was being celebrated in such a spectacular and heartfelt way. She told us, "I was confident this is what John would experience in heaven. That night was a glimpse of a place where the intrinsic worth of every person, beyond diagnosis or ability, is seen and celebrated."

But John's night didn't end there. The moment he and his mom stepped into the grand ballroom, where elegantly decorated tables framed a spacious dance floor, John's tantrum continued. But something caught Abigail's eyes. Sitting at the top of each place setting was a slice of chocolate cake—John's absolute favorite treat in the world. Immediately after John saw the chocolate cake, the tears and the screaming stopped. His eyes grew wide and a smile stretched across his face. Even though dessert wouldn't be officially served until an hour or two later, John devoured the cake. The rest is history. John had a blast. He was loved. He was celebrated. And for the first time in public, he was seen exactly the way God sees him—as royalty.

THE JOY AND THE BURDEN

Bearing the sacred responsibility of recognizing the worth in the marginalized and advocating for those who are overlooked, unnoticed, or ignored means more than laying out a red carpet or celebrating people with special needs one day of the year. It invites action on our part every single day.

God's love for humanity compels us to fight for the MVP, just as He does.

The Bible tells us that the joy of the Lord is our strength

(Nehemiah 8:10). Every day we get to wake up is a new opportunity to serve Him. What a privilege and a joy. Think about it, God invites us to play a role in His mission to care for the MVP. He doesn't need our help but chooses to partner with us to make a difference. He didn't have to, but He did. By making His mission personal, He calls us to make it personal too. This means that what we do matters. Purpose is always at play.

This joy is undeniable, yet alongside it remains a burden: the weight of our hearts breaking for the people whose hearts are broken. The crushed in spirit. The exploited. The abandoned. The unloved. The abused. The burden is heavy, reflecting the responsibility and the privilege of stewarding our lives for a purpose greater than comfort or preference.

Both joy and burden are interwoven into the fabric of humanity. Sure, pretty much all of us would prefer sticking with the joy part—it's easier and feels better—but on this side of heaven, we encounter both. In 2025, we celebrated our biggest year of Night to Shine. More than 189,000 volunteers in 822 churches in 63 countries (and all 50 states) honored more than 107,000 individuals with special needs.

There was much to celebrate! Alongside the joy, however, came sorrow. That night we were notified that one of the human trafficking survivors we served passed away. When I was told the devastating news, my heart sank. A flood of questions overwhelmed me as I wondered what I could have done or done better to prevent the tragedy.

The tension between the joy of lives transformed and the burden of impacting as many people as possible is part of the calling we embrace. This is why the apostle Paul could simultaneously say, "I consider my life worth nothing to me; my only aim is to finish the race and complete the task the Lord Jesus has given me" in Acts 20:24 (the burden), *and* "Rejoice in the Lord always. I will say it again:

Rejoice! ... Do not be anxious about anything, but in every situation, by prayer and petition, with thanksgiving, present your requests to God" in Philippians 4:4 and verse 6 (joy).

It might seem like a burden, but it's actually a reminder of how much God cares for us—that our choices truly matter. He gives us both the joy and the weight of responsibility because He invites us to live lives of purpose—not just for today but for eternity. The burden should fuel mission living and fight complacency. The joy should satisfy our efforts and motivate us to do more.

AN UNFORGETTABLE PICTURE

Every now and then, I have the privilege of stepping back and seeing what we at the foundation get to be a part of. NTS 2024 was one of those moments.

Lara is a survivor who had recently been brought into freedom thanks to one of our teams. On the morning of NTS, she shared her story of trauma and abuse with some people on our team. When you hear a cry rising from the depths of someone who has endured years of unimaginable abuse, it can stay with you forever. That cry, haunted by emotions so raw they defy words, is unlike any other. Lara's words swelled to a harrowing wail that reverberated through the heavy stillness of a room. No one dared to move. Our team, led by Demi, did what we could to comfort her. But as Lara's cries softened to a quiet whimper and her trembling shoulders stilled, none of us knew what to say.

Hours later, I watched her step off one of the buses that transported some of our guests, ready to serve as volunteer paparazzi. A trafficking operative named Marco, who was on the team that had brought Lara to freedom, was with her. A stoic individual, Marco began his faith journey as a teenager by accepting an invitation to a local church. Homeless at the time, he showed up at the church for the promise of pizza. Throughout his unique personal and professional history fighting evil, Marco has experienced and witnessed a lot of pain.

When Lara and Marco stepped off the bus that evening, both appeared a bit withdrawn. Though they were anxious to serve, neither knew what to expect at an NTS celebration. As guests arrived, Lara and Marco wondered what to do. *Clap? Shout?* They hesitated at first but, with a little encouragement, they joined us in cheering for our kings and queens. Before I knew it, Marco's eyes were lit up as he pushed children in wheelchairs and carried others in his arms down the red carpet.

But my gaze was soon captured by something else. Typically, nothing can compete for my attention when honored guests walk down the red carpet, but I was torn on this night. I took a wide turn to see the scene from a broader angle, literally stepping back to take it all in. Witnessing the mission of NTS in action, hundreds of volunteers, spanning three generations, gathering in Latin America, standing shoulder to shoulder with the kings and queens of the night—wow! It was one of the clearest depictions of heaven's joy on earth, the same picture John's mom had described. Everyone celebrating everyone.

Shifting my focus back to Lara and Marco, the picture only became clearer. Seeing a girl who was once trafficked and tormented now shining as brightly as our guests was a powerful reminder of God's love and perspective. The night wasn't just about shining a light on others, it was about God lighting one within her. I believe for the first time Lara began to see herself as God sees her. Worthy. Valuable.

A queen. And Marco? Here was a freedom fighter who had seen more darkness than I can ever imagine, fully invested in celebrating the people many have forgotten.

Isn't it just like God to transform a morning filled with trauma-laced reminders into a night of sweet celebration, a night where God's image is both celebrating and being celebrated?

This living picture of hope realized is exactly why we strive to visit the poor, the brokenhearted, the captives, and all who mourn (Isaiah 61:1).

It's why we try to go out of our way, going the distance to show MVPs that they have royal worth.

It's why we take seriously and embrace our royalty as God's representative instead of seeking comfort and indulgence.

It's why we break down the door.

It's why we don't just say that every human being has royal worth, we live like it's true.

It's why we choose to trade apathy for action.

It's why we don't let the tension between joy and burden tempt us to quit or "become weary in doing good" (Galatians 6:9).

It's why we look again and see a diamond instead of a pebble.

It's why we run into, not away from, darkness.

REST IS BIBLICAL AND SO IS *RUNNING*

The Greek word for run, *trecho* (treh'-o), is used twenty times in seventeen verses in the New Testament.[6] Following are a few examples:

- So the women hurried away from the tomb, afraid yet filled with joy, and *ran* to tell his disciples. (Matthew 28:8)

- When he saw Jesus from a distance, he *ran* and fell on his knees in front of him. (Mark 5:6)
- Peter, however, got up and *ran* to the tomb. Bending over, he saw the strips of linen lying by themselves, and he went away, wondering to himself what had happened. (Luke 24:12)
- Do you not know that all the runners in a stadium compete, but only one receives the prize? So *run* to win. (1 Corinthians 9:24 NET)

Trecho denotes an urgency, advancing speedily like an athlete competing in the ancient Greek games. It's moving forward with full effort and directed purpose.

Let me ask you something: Why do we run? Why do we push ourselves, strain every muscle, and sprint toward a life of purpose? The answer is simple: Because God calls us to. Because people are worth it. Because our time here on earth is short. Because we don't want to live on our timeline but on the timeline of those lost in darkness.

We don't run because we have the perfect strategy or have the intellectual answer to every question. We run because every single person is created as God's image and is worth the life, death, and resurrection of His Son, Jesus Christ.

Running isn't about perfection but about the willingness to see people the way God sees them. He viewed them as worth dying for, so are they worth enough for me to strain, to sweat for them? Do I see people as valuable enough to act? To run? I don't have an excuse. I've been told. I know their value. The test isn't whether I understand it; it's what I'm going to do about it. I don't want to stand before God and say, "I didn't realize how much people were worth running for"; I want to strive to live in a way that proves I do. I know I fall short. And I know

I'll mess up along the way, but that's okay. This isn't about expertise; it's about effort.

Too many of us spend our lives standing still, critiquing, or casually walking toward a calling that demands a full-out sprint. The Bible is full of moments when people ran. The possessed man ran to Jesus. The father in the parable of the prodigal son ran to his child. The women ran from the empty tomb, and John ran to see it for himself. Paul talked about running with intensity to win others to Christ. Even Jesus ran His race with endurance, enduring the cross for the joy set before Him.

If the gospel is personal to Jesus, it should be personal to us. Think about it. If a girl is being trafficked 5.3 times a day, shouldn't it light a fire in us to get to her before she has to endure one more moment of pain? If a child is abandoned, shouldn't we run to him like our lives depend on it? We can't be content to stand still while the world around us is crying out for hope.

> If the gospel is personal to Jesus, it should be personal to us.

And yes, people might call this exhausting. They might say, "That's intense," or "That's not sustainable." But if we truly believe what we claim to believe, then how can we not run? How can we not strain every fiber of our being for the sake of others?

When you show up to heaven, how do you want to arrive? Do you want to say, "Man, I had forty years of great rest and took a lot of naps"? Or do you want to stand before Jesus, sweaty, battered, and dog-tired because you gave everything you had? I know which one I'd choose. I want to show up to heaven exhausted!

Rest has its place, but let's not let it become our default. Let's run. Let's strain. Let's show up to heaven with nothing left in the tank because we poured it all out for the mission.

The hurting, the helpless, and the hopeless are waiting. The lost are waiting. Will you run with me? It starts by looking again—at ourselves, at one another, at the vulnerable. At *Jesus*.

On your mark. Get set. Go!

> Let's show up to heaven with nothing left in the tank because we poured it all out for the mission.

ACKNOWLEDGMENTS

DEMI, THANK YOU FOR BEING THE ONE WHO CON-stantly helps me "look again." From that moment at the NTS, when we saw the sticker that sparked this journey, to every step along the way, you've helped me see people and purpose more clearly.

To Mom and Dad, You model what it means to truly look again and to see others through the eyes of Jesus. Thank you.

To the whole team at the Tim Tebow Foundation and The Tebow Group, thank you for not only believing in this message but for showing up daily and working diligently to live it out.

Wyatt, you've played an instrumental role in helping make this book a reality. Your heart for the gospel and your love for theology has sharpened my own. Thank you for your passion for this message and challenging me to dig deeper and ask the right questions.

Andrew, thank you for believing in this book from the beginning. Your hope in this message and your steady leadership helped bring *Look Again* to life in a powerful way.

Paul, thank you for walking with us through every twist and turn. Your patience, insight, and craftsmanship helped carry this book across the finish line.

Thank you to Dr. Michael Bird, Dr. Carmen Imes, Dr. Catherine McDowell, Dr. Craig Blomberg, Dr. Tremper Longman III, and

Dr. Paul Copan for taking time to speak with me and my team. Your insights were incredibly valuable in the development of this book. I am so grateful for each of your ministries.

AJ Gregory, every time we work on a new book I value and appreciate your skill and talent deeper. Thank you for all the ways you care so deeply about the mission of this message and helping this dyslexic author bring a book to reality.

Tommy Martin, your heart for fueling and amplifying faith, hope, and love is one of the countless reasons Demi and I value your leadership and friendship. Thank you for living out your calling daily, and inspiring those around you to do the same.

To the Thomas Nelson team, it's an honor to work alongside you. Thank you for your diligence and professionalism throughout this process.

NOTES

Introduction
1. "Science Highlights," NASA, last updated April 9, 2025, https://science.nasa.gov/mission/hubble/science/science-highlights/.
2. Richard Hollingham, "The Spacewalk That Saved Hubble," BBC, September 23, 2015, https://www.bbc.com/future/article/20150423-the-man-who-made-hubble-see.
3. Dennis Overbye, "25 Years Later, Hubble Sees Beyond Troubled Start," *New York Times*, April 24, 2015, https://www.nytimes.com/2015/04/24/science/25-years-later-hubble-sees-beyond-troubled-start.html.
4. Richard Speed, "Remember When the Hubble Space Telescope Was More Punchline Than Science Powerhouse?," *Register*, December 3, 2023, https://www.theregister.com/2023/12/04/remember_when_the_hubble_space/.
5. John A. Logsdon, "Return to Flight: Richard H. Truly and the Recovery from the *Challenger* Accident," in *From Engineering Science to Big Science: The NACA and NASA Collier Trophy Research Project Winners*, ed. Pamela E. Mack (NASA History Division, 1998), 345–64, https://www.nasa.gov/history/SP-4219/Chapter15.html.
6. Hollingham, "Spacewalk That Saved Hubble."

Chapter 1: Life Unworthy of Life
1. Tim Tebow and Loretta Claiborne, "'U.S.' Claiborne Gives Inspiring Advice During Opening Ceremony," ESPN video, 2 min., 3 sec., https://www.espn.com/video/clip/_/id/37869451.

Notes

2. Zach Smith, "Going for Gold," *Rural Missouri*, May 15, 2023, https://ruralmissouri.org/going-for-gold/.
3. "Charlie Phillips Wins Four Medals at Special Olympics World Games Berlin," *Sun Times News*, June 26, 2023, https://suntimesnews.com/2023/06/26/charlie-phillips-wins-four-medals-at-special-olympics-world-games-berlin/.
4. Special Olympics (@specialolympics), "The @sowg_berlin2023 have been lit up by athletes," Instagram, June 24, 2023, https://www.instagram.com/specialolympics/reel/Ct4PXB_NBBk/.
5. "Special Olympics World Games Berlin 2023," Special Olympics, accessed May 2, 2025, https://www.specialolympics.org/stories/news/special-olympics-world-games-berlin-2023#.
6. Adolf Hitler, "Weltanschauung and Party," in *Mein Kampf* [My struggle], vol. 2, *The National Socialist Movement*, trans. James Murphy (Hurst and Blackett, 1939), 322, https://archive.org/details/in.ernet.dli.2015.526617/page/n323/mode/2up.
7. William Frederick Meinecke Jr., *Nazi Ideology and the Holocaust* (United States Holocaust Memorial Museum, 2007), 81–82, https://www.ushmm.org/m/pdfs/20090831-nazi-ideology-book-part2.pdf.
8. Mark P. Mostert, "Useless Eaters: Disability as Genocidal Marker in Nazi Germany," *The Journal of Special Education* 36, no. 3 (2002): 155–68, http://courses.washington.edu/intro2ds/Readings/Mostert%20Useless%20Eaters.pdf.
9. Karl Binding and Alfred Hoche, *Allowing the Destruction of Life Unworthy of Life: Its Measure and Form*, trans. Cristina Modak (Suzeteo Enterprises, 2015), Kindle.
10. Binding and Hoche, *Allowing the Destruction of Life*.
11. Gene Edward Veith, *Modern Fascism: The Threat to the Judeo-Christian Worldview* (Concordia, 1993), Kindle.
12. Anthony Horvath, "Life Unworthy of Life Yesterday and Today, Science, Secularism, and the Sanctity of Life," foreword to Binding and Hoche, *Allowing the Destruction of Life*, Eugenics Archive, accessed June 26, 2025, https://eugenicsarchive.com/life-unworthy-of-life-yesterday-and-today-science-secularism-and-the-sanctity-of-life/120.htm.
13. Binding and Hoche, *Allowing the Destruction of Life*.
14. Binding and Hoche, *Allowing the Destruction of Life*.

15. United States Holocaust Memorial Museum, "The Biological State: Nazi Racial Hygiene, 1933–1939," Holocaust Encyclopedia, accessed May 2, 2025, https://encyclopedia.ushmm.org/content/en/article/the-biological-state-nazi-racial-hygiene-1933-1939; Robert Proctor, "The Sterilization Law," in *Racial Hygiene: Medicine Under the Nazis* (Harvard University Press, 1988), 95–117.
16. Paul Weindling, "The Dangers of White Supremacy: Nazi Sterilization and Its Mixed-Race Adolescent Victims," *American Journal of Public Health* 112, no. 2 (2022): 248–54, https://doi.org/10.2105/AJPH.2021.306593.
17. Alexandra Minna Stern, "Forced Sterilization Policies in the US Targeted Minorities and Those with Disabilities and Lasted into the 21st Century, *The Conversation*, August 26, 2020, https://theconversation.com/forced-sterilization-policies-in-the-us-targeted-minorities-and-those-with-disabilities-and-lasted-into-the-21st-century-143144.
18. https://theconversation.com/forced-sterilization-policies-in-the-us-targeted-minorities-and-those-with-disabilities-and-lasted-into-the-21st-century-143144.
19. Linda Villarosa, "The Long Shadow of Eugenics in America," *New York Times Magazine*, June 8, 2022, https://www.nytimes.com/2022/06/08/magazine/eugenics-movement-america.html.
20. United States Holocaust Memorial Museum, "Eugenics," Holocaust Encyclopedia, accessed May 2, 2025, https://encyclopedia.ushmm.org/content/en/article/eugenics.
21. Villarosa, "Long Shadow of Eugenics in America."
22. Sara Hanafi, "Research Ethics in the 20th Century: The History of Research Ethics in 20th Century Nazi Germany and WWII," November 21, 2023, https://storymaps.arcgis.com/stories/c85290c0c51c4c6f8a29ecc381be6b56.
23. Raj Bhopal, "Hitler on Race and Health in *Mein Kampf*: A Stimulus to Anti-Racism in the Health Professions," *Diversity and Equality in Health and Care* 2, no. 2 (2005): 119–25, https://era.ed.ac.uk/bitstream/handle/1842/3057/hitler.pdf?sequence=1&isAllowed=y.
24. United States Holocaust Memorial Museum, "Euthanasia Program and

Notes

Aktion T4," Holocaust Encyclopedia, accessed May 2, 2025, https://encyclopedia.ushmm.org/content/en/article/euthanasia-program.
25. United States Holocaust Memorial Museum, "Euthanasia Program."
26. Henry Friedlander, *The Origins of Nazi Genocide: From Euthanasia to the Final Solution* (University of North Carolina Press, 1997), 45.
27. Friedlander, *Origins of Nazi Genocide*, 59, 46.
28. Friedlander, 50.
29. Friedlander, 50.
30. Friedlander, 48.
31. Patricia Heberer Rice, "Disability Awareness Month: The Nazis' Nameless Victims," moderated by Edna Friedberg, posted October 30, 2020, by United States Holocaust Memorial Museum, YouTube, 36 min., 10 sec., https://www.youtube.com/watch?v=uvrwnJ6hQ9s.
32. Lutz Kaelber, "Jewish Children with Disabilities and Nazi 'Euthanasia' Crimes," *Bulletin of the Carolyn and Leonard Miller Center for Holocaust Studies* 17 (Spring 2013): 1, https://www.uvm.edu/~lkaelber/bull2013-Kaelber1.pdf.
33. Kaelber, "Nazi 'Euthanasia,'" 21.
34. United States Holocaust Memorial Museum, "'Euthanasia' Propaganda," State of Deception: The Power of Nazi Propaganda, accessed June 26, 2025, https://exhibitions.ushmm.org/propaganda/euthanasia-propaganda.
35. Friedlander, *Origins of Nazi Genocide*, 75.
36. Kenny Fries, "Before the 'Final Solution' There Was a 'Test Killing,'" *New York Times*, January 8, 2020, https://www.nytimes.com/2020/01/08/opinion/disability-nazi-eugenics.html; Veith, *Modern Fascism*.
37. Vivien Spitz, *Doctors from Hell: The Horrific Account of Nazi Experiments on Humans* (Sentient, 2005), Kindle.
38. Dagmar Herzog, *The Question of Unworthy Life: Eugenics and Germany's Twentieth Century* (Princeton University Press, 2024), Kindle.
39. Friedlander, *Origins of Nazi Genocide*, 95–96.
40. Friedlander, 101–2.
41. Friedlander, 95.
42. Friedlander, 95.
43. Friedlander, 96.
44. Sarah Handley-Cousins, host, *Dig: A History Podcast*, podcast, "Life

Unworthy of Life: The Nazi Programs to Kill People with Disabilities," May 19, 2019, https://digpodcast.org/2019/05/19/nazi-eugenics/.
45. Fries, "Before the 'Final Solution.'"
46. Veith, *Modern Fascism*.
47. Disability Rights Advocates, *Forgotten Crimes: The Holocaust and People with Disabilities* (Disability Rights Advocates, 2001), https://www.canonsociaalwerk.eu/1943_apeldoorn/forgotten_crimes.pdf.
48. "Etymology of 'Renew,'" Etymonline, accessed May 2, 2025, https://www.etymonline.com/word/renew.

Chapter 2: Image Is Everything

1. Catherine McDowell, "An Old Testament Theology of the Image," from the Wheaton College Theology Conference, posted April 10, 2015, by Wheaton College, YouTube, 35 min., 19 sec., https://www.youtube.com/watch?v=d8G1p_4ycrI.
2. To be clear, the Bible doesn't tell us exactly what the phrase "image of God" means. According to the late linguist John F. A. Sawyer, either the author was referring to something so well known to his original audience that he didn't need to explain it or the author believed it to be of less importance than we make it out to be. John F. A. Sawyer, "The Meaning of סיה לֶא םֶלֶצְבּ ('In the Image of God') in Genesis I–XI," *Journal of Theological Studies* 25, no. 2 (1974): 426, http://www.jstor.org/stable/23958411.
3. The rational view is also referred to as the substantive or structural view.

Chapter 3: The Truth of Who We Are

1. James Strong, *A Concise Dictionary of the Words in the Greek Testament and the Hebrew Bible* (Logos Bible Software, 2009), 70.
2. "Mephibosheth," Precept Austin, last updated March 22, 2023, https://www.preceptaustin.org/mephibosheth.
3. "What Is the Significance of Lo Debar in the Bible?," Got Questions, last updated January 4, 2022, https://www.gotquestions.org/Lo-Debar-in-the-Bible.html.
4. John 9:1–3.
5. Exodus 4.
6. David L. Turner, "Image of God," Bible Study Tools, accessed May 2, 2025,

Notes

      https://www.biblestudytools.com/dictionaries/bakers-evangelical-dictionary/image-of-god.html.

7. Kenneth A. Mathews, *The New American Commentary*, vol. 1, *Genesis 1–11:26* (Broadman & Holman, 1996), 168; Carmen Joy Imes, *Being God's Image: Why Creation Still Matters* (InterVarsity Press, 2023), 31.
8. G. K. Beale et al., eds., *Dictionary of the New Testament Use of the Old Testament* (Baker Academic, 2023), 349.
9. Another "image of God" passage does exist in Genesis 9:6, just not "image" and "likeness" together.
10. Catherine McDowell, "An Old Testament Theology of the Image," from the Wheaton College Theology Conference, posted April 10, 2015, by Wheaton College, YouTube, 35 min., 19 sec., www.youtube.com/watch?v=d8G1p_4ycrI.

Chapter 4: Our Royal Reality

1. Dan Witters, "U.S. Depression Rates Reach New Highs," Gallup, May 17, 2023, https://news.gallup.com/poll/505745/depression-rates-reach-new-highs.aspx.
2. Witters, "U.S. Depression Rates."
3. The Dipex Charity, "Depression, Sense of Self and Self-Esteem," HealthTalk.org, accessed May 2, 2025, https://healthtalk.org/experiences/depression-and-low-mood/depression-self-and-self-esteem/.
4. Richard Weissbourd et al., "On Edge: Understanding and Preventing Young Adults' Mental Health Challenges," Harvard Graduate School of Education, October 2023, https://mcc.gse.harvard.edu/reports/on-edge.
5. "Suicide," World Health Organization, March 25, 2025, https://www.who.int/news-room/fact-sheets/detail/suicide.
6. Francesca Aton, "Rembrandt's *The Standard Bearer* Debuts at the Rijksmuseum with Free Entry," Art News, June 16, 2023, https://www.artnews.com/art-news/news/rembrandt-the-standard-bearer-debuts-at-the-rijksmuseum-with-free-entry-1234671869/.
7. "What Did Jesus Mean When He Promised an Abundant Life?," Got Questions, last updated January 4, 2022, https://www.gotquestions.org/abundant-life.html.
8. Kenneth A. Mathews, *The New American Commentary: Genesis 1–11:26*, vol. 1 (Broadman & Holman, 1996), 195–96.

9. Genesis 1:12, 21, 24, 25 NASB.
10. Paul David Tripp, *Do You Believe? 12 Historic Doctrines to Change Your Everyday Life* (Crossway, 2021), 230.
11. Hebrews 2:7–9; Colossians 1:15.
12. Christopher Watkin, *Biblical Critical Theory: How the Bible's Unfolding Story Makes Sense of Modern Life and Culture* (Zondervan, 2022), 92–93.

Chapter 5: When Royalty Goes Wrong

1. "Sanctuary of Christ the Redeemer," Google Arts and Culture, accessed May 2, 2025, https://g.co/arts/rm9HjcTvZ7SUuTkL8; Jeff Wells, "11 Facts About Rio's Christ the Redeemer Statue," Mental Floss, August 11, 2016, https://www.mentalfloss.com/article/84546/11-facts-about-rios-christ-redeemer-statue.
2. Jeffrey Overstreet, "Trash Transformed," *Image*, November 30, 2010, https://imagejournal.org/2010/11/30/trash-transformed/.
3. Marilia Brocchetto and Azadeh Ansari, "Landfill's Closure Changing Lives in Rio," CNN, June 5, 2012, https://www.cnn.com/2012/06/05/world/americas/brazil-landfill-closure/index.html.
4. Cynthia Fuchs, "'Waste Land': Another Reality," Pop Matters, November 1, 2010, https://www.popmatters.com/132980-waste-land-2496116848.html.
5. Lisa Rabey, "Waste Land—UICA Films Review," The Rapidian, February 26, 2011, https://therapidian.org/waste-land-uica-films-review.
6. Felicity Clarke, "Waste Land Pickers Struggle from Landfill Closure," Rio on Watch, June 21, 2012, https://rioonwatch.org/?p=4032.
7. Kathleen M. Millar, "The Precarious Present: Wageless Labor and Disrupted Life in Rio de Janeiro, Brazil," *Cultural Anthropology* 29, no. 1 (2014): 32–53, https://doi.org/10.14506/ca29.1.04.
8. Beatriz Santos, "PET Recycling in Brazil," Sustainable Plastics, October 11, 2023, https://www.sustainableplastics.com/news/pet-recycling-brazil#.
9. Eoghan Macguire and Sofia Fernandes, "From Garbage to Gold: Brazil's Catadores Turn Trash into Art," CNN World, June 13, 2013, https://www.cnn.com/2013/06/12/world/brazil-catadores-trash-treasure/index.html.
10. Steve Murray, "Review: 'Waste Land,' Deeply Moving, Finds Art and Dignity Among Brazil's Poorest," ArtsATL, November 19, 2010, https://www.artsatl.org/film-review-waste-land-deeply-moving-finds-art-dignity-and-life-among-brazils-poorest/.

11. Millar, "Precarious Present."
12. Millar, "Precarious Present."
13. Aaron Armstrong, "What Does 'Missing the Mark' Mean? [99 in :99]," Lifeway, August 26, 2020, https://gospelproject.lifeway.com/sin-missing-mark-video/.
14. "How Big of a Problem Is Human Trafficking?," Our Rescue, June 21, 2023, https://ourrescue.org/education/prevention-awareness/how-big-of-a-problem-is-human-trafficking.
15. "Oldsmar Man Pleads Guilty to Producing and Distributing Child Sexual Abuse and AI-Generated Child Sexual Abuse Material," US Attorney's Office, Middle District of Florida, press release, December 6, 2024, https://www.justice.gov/usao-mdfl/pr/oldsmar-man-pleads-guilty-producing-and-distributing-child-sexual-abuse-and-ai.
16. Jeff Rosenfield, "Federal Child Porn Arrest Sending 'Shock Waves' Through Oldsmar," *Tampa Bay Times*, October 23, 2023, https://www.tampabay.com/news/crime/2023/10/23/federal-child-porn-arrest-sending-shockwaves-through-oldsmar/.
17. "Sexual Misconduct," Southern Connecticut State University, accessed May 2, 2025, https://inside.southernct.edu/sexual-misconduct/facts.
18. Carmen Joy Imes, *Being God's Image: Why Creation Still Matters* (InterVarsity Press, 2023), 53.
19. Imes, *Being God's Image*, 54.
20. "Isabel, Princess Imperial of Brazil," Google Arts and Culture, accessed May 2, 2025, https://artsandculture.google.com/entity/isabel-princess-imperial-of-brazil/m06rdk7?hl=en#.
21. Colin M. Snider, "Get to Know a Brazilian—Princess Isabel," *Americas South and North* (blog), September 2, 2012, https://americasouthandnorth.wordpress.com/2012/09/02/get-to-know-a-brazilian-princess-isabel/.
22. Alyssa Murphy, "Celebrating Christ the King: 12 Interesting Facts About Christ the Redeemer Statue," *National Catholic Register*, November 26, 2023, https://www.ncregister.com/blog/celebrating-christ-the-king-12-interesting-facts-about-christ-the-redeemer-statue.
23. "Sanctuary of Christ the Redeemer," Google Arts and Culture.
24. "Sanctuary of Christ the Redeemer," Google Arts and Culture.

Chapter 6: The Royal Rescue
1. Josh McDowell, *More Than a Carpenter* (1977; repr., Tyndale Elevate, 2011), 154–55.
2. McDowell, *More Than a Carpenter*, 154–55.
3. *Strong's Lexicon*, "2098. euangelion," Bible Hub, accessed May 2, 2025, https://biblehub.com/greek/2098.htm.
4. Kenneth E. Bailey, *Jesus Through Middle Eastern Eyes: Cultural Studies in the Gospels* (InterVarsity Press, 2008), 35, https://www.ivpress.com/Media/Default/Downloads/Excerpts-and-Samples/2568-excerpt.pdf.
5. C. S. Lewis, *Miracles: A Preliminary Study* (Macmillan, 1947), 237.
6. Personal conversation.
7. *Strong's Lexicon*, "2644. katallassó," Bible Hub, accessed May 2, 2025, https://biblehub.com/greek/2644.htm.
8. "Greek Speak: Katallassō," Christian Standard Bible: CSB News and Information, August 19, 2021, https://csbible.com/greek-speak-katallasso/.
9. Matthew Williams, "The Prodigal Son's Father Shouldn't Have Run! Putting Luke 15:11–32 in Context," *Biola Magazine*, May 31, 2010, https://www.biola.edu/blogs/biola-magazine/2010/the-prodigal-sons-father-shouldnt-have-run.
10. Williams, "Prodigal Son's Father."
11. *Strong's Lexicon*, "splagchnizomai," Blue Letter Bible, accessed May 2, 2025, https://www.blueletterbible.org/lexicon/g4697/kjv/tr/0-1/.

Chapter 7: What Our Royal Status Means
1. Jennifer Dobson, "An Adoption Aid Story: The Family of Eternal Love," Tim Tebow Foundation, accessed June 26, 2025, https://timtebowfoundation.org/stories/adoption-aid-story-family-eternal-love.
2. Imes, *Being God's Image*, 6.
3. Dictionary.com, "bear," accessed May 2, 2025, https://www.dictionary.com/browse/bear.
4. Imes, *Being God's Image*, 54.
5. Bethany Verrett, "Why Does God Call Himself 'I Am Who I Am'?," Bible Study Tools, February 22, 2023, https://www.biblestudytools.com/bible-study/topical-studies/why-does-god-call-himself-i-am-that-i-am.html.
6. Carrie Arnold, "See the Amazing Way a Beetle Survives Being Eaten,"

National Geographic, February 6, 2018, https://www.nationalgeographic.com/animals/article/beetle-survives-toad-vomit-animals.
7. "Bombardier Beetles," *National Geographic*, accessed May 2, 2025, https://www.nationalgeographic.com/animals/invertebrates/facts/bombardier-beetle.
8. Arnold, "See the Amazing Way a Beetle Survives Being Eaten."
9. Dr. Henry Richter and David Coppedge, *Spacecraft Earth: A Guide for Passengers* (Creation Book Publishers, 2017), 110.
10. "Bombardier Beetles," *National Geographic*.
11. "Current World Population," Worldometer, accessed May 2, 2025, https://www.worldometers.info/world-population.
12. Jonathan Jarry, "Identical Twins Are Not Identical," Office for Science and Society, McGill University, January 21, 2021, https://www.mcgill.ca/oss/article/general-science/identical-twins-are-not-identical.
13. Michael J. Kruger, "How Early Christianity Was Mocked for Welcoming Women," Canon Fodder, July 13, 2020, https://michaeljkruger.com/how-early-christianity-was-mocked-for-welcoming-women/.
14. Tom Holland, *Dominion: How the Christian Revolution Remade the World* (Basic Books, 2021).
15. John S. Dickerson, *Jesus Skeptic: A Journalist Explores the Credibility and Impact of Christianity* (Baker Books, 2019), 177.
16. Permission granted to use portion of sermon.

Chapter 8: Jesus in the Margins
1. "Man Sees Color for the First Time," posted September 16, 2017, by Poke My Heart, YouTube, 1 min., 18 sec., https://www.youtube.com/watch?app=desktop&v=1ZcK-Eima-w.
2. *Collins Dictionary*, "margin," accessed May 2, 2025, https://www.collinsdictionary.com/us/dictionary/english/margin#.
3. Irmo Marini, "The History of Treatment Toward People with Disabilities," in *Psychosocial Aspects of Disability*, 2nd ed., ed. Irmo Marini et al. (Springer, 2017), https://connect.springerpub.com/content/book/978-0-8261-8063-6/part/part01/chapter/ch01.
4. Narry F. Santos, "Jesus' Mission to the Vulnerable: The Power of Servanthood in the Gospel of Mark," *Evangelical Review of Theology: A*

Global Forum 48, no. 1 (February 2024): 30–39, https://theology.worldea.org/wp-content/uploads/2024/01/ERT-48-1_web.pdf.
5. Santos, "Jesus' Mission to the Vulnerable," 32–33, 34.
6. Not including implicit mentions (he "found" the disciples sleeping [Matthew 26:40]).
7. John 20:16.
8. Alan L. Gillen, "Biblical Leprosy: Shedding Light on the Disease That Shuns," Answers in Genesis, June 10, 2007, https://answersingenesis.org/biology/disease/biblical-leprosy-shedding-light-on-the-disease-that-shuns; *Strong's Lexicon*, "3014. lepra," Bible Hub, accessed May 2, 2025, https://biblehub.com/greek/3014.htm.
9. "Why Is Leprosy Talked About So Much in the Bible?," Got Questions, last updated January 4, 2022, https://www.gotquestions.org/Bible-leprosy.html.
10. Leviticus 13:45; Francois P. Viljoen, "Jesus Healing the Leper and the Purity Law in the Gospel of Matthew," *In Skriflig (Online)* 48, no. 2 (2014): 1–7, https://scielo.org.za/scielo.php?script=sci_arttext&pid=S2305-08532014000200004.
11. David Guzik, "Luke 5—Disciples Are Called," Enduring Word, accessed May 2, 2025, https://enduringword.com/bible-commentary/luke-5/.
12. *NASB Lexicon*, "Mark 1:41," Bible Hub, accessed May 2, 2025, https://biblehub.com/lexicon/mark/1-41.htm.
13. Personal conversation.
14. "60 Fascinating Facts About the Queen's Coronation," Royal Central, June 1, 2013, https://royalcentral.co.uk/features/history-blogs/coronationfacts-8604/.
15. "50 Facts About Queen Elizabeth II's Coronation," The Royal Household, accessed May 7, 2025, https://www.royal.uk/50-facts-about-queen-elizabeth-iis-coronation; "The Coronation of Queen Elizabeth II, 1953," London Museum, accessed May 2, 2025, https://www.londonmuseum.org.uk/collections/london-stories/the-coronation-of-queen-elizabeth-ii-1953/; "60 Fascinating Facts," Royal Central.
16. "60 Fascinating Facts," Royal Central.
17. "From the Archives: Queen Salote of Tonga," Royal Over-Seas League, February 22, 2018, https://rosl.org.uk/from-the-archives-queen-salote-of-tonga/.

Notes

Chapter 9: God's Image—No Exceptions

1. Susan M. Schweik, *The Ugly Laws: Disability in Public* (New York University Press, 2009), 2.
2. Susan M. Schweik and Robert A. Wilson, "Ugly Laws," PhilArchive, accessed June 26, 2025, https://philarchive.org/archive/SCHUL.
3. Schweik, *Ugly Laws*, 291.
4. Schweik, 291–96.
5. Schweik, 3, 4.
6. Schweik, 2.
7. Schweik and Wilson, "Ugly Laws."
8. Ainsley Hawthorn, "Illegal to Be 'Ugly'? The History Behind One of America's Cruelest Laws," *National Geographic*, August 9, 2024, https://www.nationalgeographic.com/history/article/history-of-ugly-laws-america-disability.
9. Schweik, *Ugly Laws*, 33.
10. Hawthorn, "Illegal to Be 'Ugly'?"
11. Schweik, *Ugly Laws*, 293.
12. Schweik, 1.
13. Schweik, 293.
14. Livia Gershon, "The Ugly History of Chicago's 'Ugly Law,'" *JSTOR Daily*, September 3, 2021, https://daily.jstor.org/the-ugly-history-of-chicagos-ugly-law/.
15. Schweik, *Ugly Laws*, 1–2.
16. Schweik, 6.
17. Elizabeth Greiwe, "Chicago's 'Ugly Law,'" *Chicago Tribune*, digital edition, accessed May 2, 2025, https://digitaledition.chicagotribune.com/tribune/article_popover.aspx?guid=61665d57-20c0-4440-8d8b-717ec2b7fcc9.
18. "Disability," World Health Organization, March 7, 2023, https://www.who.int/news-room/fact-sheets/detail/disability-and-health.
19. Gershon, "Ugly History."

Chapter 10: Royalty in Rubble

1. "Human Trafficking," US Department of Justice, accessed May 6, 2025, https://www.justice.gov/humantrafficking; International Labour Organization, *Global Estimates of Modern Slavery: Forced Labour and Forced Marriage* (2022), https://www.alliance87.org/sites/default

/files/2023-06/Global%20Estimates%20of%20Modern%20Slavery%20Forced%20Labour%20and%20Forced%20Marriage_0.pdf.
2. Heather Komenda, "Despite Progress, More Needs to Be Done to Address the Crime of Trafficking in Persons," United Nations, July 24, 2023, https://www.un.org/en/un-chronicle/despite-progress-more-needs-be-done-address-crime-trafficking-persons.
3. *Polaris Analysis of 2021 Data from the National Human Trafficking Hotline* (Polaris, 2022), https://polarisproject.org/wp-content/uploads/2020/07/Polaris-Analysis-of-2021-Data-from-the-National-Human-Trafficking-Hotline.pdf.
4. UN Special Representative of the Secretary-General on Violence Against Children, "SRSG on Violence Against Children Joins ICAT in Calling on Governments to Reach Every Victim of Trafficking, Leaving No One Behind," United Nations, July 30, 2023, https://violenceagainstchildren.un.org/news/srsg-violence-against-children-joins-icat-calling-governments-reach-every-victim-trafficking.
5. Rosalyn Roden, "Traffickers Taking $236 Billion in Illegal Profits at Victims' Expense," Hope for Justice, March 21, 2024, https://hopeforjustice.org/news/traffickers-taking-236-billion-in-illegal-profits-at-victims-expense/.
6. Justin Teitelbaum, "The NFL's Most Valuable Teams 2024," *Forbes*, August 29, 2024, https://www.forbes.com/sites/justinteitelbaum/2024/08/29/the-nfls-most-valuable-teams-2024/.
7. *Polaris Analysis of 2021 Data*; "Family Members Are Involved in Nearly Half of Child Trafficking Cases," International Organization for Migration, 2018, www.iom.int/sites/g/files/tmzbdl2616/files/2018-07/Counter-trafficking%20Data%20Brief%20081217.pdf.
8. Mboza Lwandiko, "Rise of Children Violence and Sexual Abuse: A Need to Raise Voices Higher," SSRN, November 16, 2023, https://papers.ssrn.com/sol3/papers.cfm?abstract_id=4635567.
9. Interpol, *Towards a Global Indicator on Unidentified Victims in Child Sexual Exploitation Material: Summary Report* (2018), https://ecpat.org/wp-content/uploads/2021/05/towards-a-global-indicator-on-unidentified-victims-in-child-sexual-exploitation-material-Summary-Report.pdf.
10. Personal communication with the author.
11. Frank Turek (@drfankturek), "Where does evil come from?," Instagram,

February 22, 2025, https://www.instagram.com/reel/DGYEGt6Py2N/?igsh=NmEzcXFrcnVkNmxu.

Chapter 11: A Royal Response

1. Middleton, *Liberating Image*, 27.
2. "Lovingkindness—Definition of *Hesed*," Precept Austin, last updated October 29, 2023, https://www.preceptaustin.org/lovingkindness-definition_of_hesed.
3. "Euangelion / Gospel," Bible Project, accessed May 2, 2025, https://bibleproject.com/explore/video/euangelion-gospel/.
4. Ethan's personal journal entry.
5. John Seidl, "The Miracle on Maui: A Stranger's Encounter with a Dying Boy Leads to Redemption and Transformation," Christian Broadcasting Network, March 4, 2024, https://cbn.com/news/us/miracle-maui-strangers-encounter-dying-boy-leads-redemption-and-transformation.
6. *The Ethan Hallmark Legacy*, 2nd ed., I Am Second (website), streaming video, accessed May 2, 2025, https://www.iamsecond.com/film/ethan-second-edition/#modal-media-vimeo.
7. Seidl, "The Miracle on Maui."
8. "Ethan's Echo of Hope: Touching Lives with Make-A-Wish," posted May 20, 2024, by Make-A-Wish North Texas, YouTube, 16 min., 6 sec., https://www.youtube.com/watch?v=X3rhXX0llO0.
9. Seidl, "The Miracle on Maui."

Chapter 12: Lives on the Line

1. Edna Hong, *Bright Valley of Love* (Postscript, 1976; repr., Concordia Theological Seminary Press, 2021), 9, 10.
2. Hong, *Bright Valley of Love*, 36.
3. Cheryl Magness, "Book About Nazi Slaughter of the Disabled Nearly Lost to History Sends a Message to Post-*Roe* America," *The Federalist*, July 19, 2022, https://thefederalist.com/2022/07/19/book-about-nazi-slaughter-of-the-disabled-nearly-lost-to-history-sends-a-message-to-post-roe-america/.
4. Magness, "Book About Nazi Slaughter."
5. Leslie Jones, "The Question of Unworthy Life," *Quarterly Review*,

November 30, 2024, http://www.quarterly-review.org/the-question-of-unworthy-life/.
6. Michael S. Bryant, "Lucifer on the Ruins of the World: The German Euthanasia Trials, 1948–1950," in *Confronting the "Good Death": Nazi Euthanasia on Trial, 1945–1953* (University Press of Colorado, 2017), https://muse.jhu.edu/pub/173/oa_monograph/chapter/2276647.
7. United States Holocaust Memorial Museum, "German Bishop Condemns the Killing of People with Disabilities," USHMM: History Unfolded, https://newspapers.ushmm.org/events/german-bishop-condemns-the-killing-of-people-with-disabilities.
8. Suzanne E. Evans, *Forgotten Crimes: The Holocaust and People with Disabilities* (Ivan R. Dee, 2023), 160.
9. cygardner19, "Infanticide and Rearing Practices in Ancient Greece," Women in Antiquity, December 1, 2020, https://womeninantiquity.wordpress.com/2020/12/01/infanticide-and-rearing-practices-in-ancient-greece/.
10. Uche Anizor, *Overcoming Apathy: Gospel Hope for Those Who Struggle to Care* (Crossway, 2022), 57.
11. Anizor, *Overcoming Apathy*, 93.
12. "Batman Begins (Clip 3): The Everlasting and Incorruptible Symbol to Protect Your Loved Ones," posted January 22, 2014, by Bruce Huang, YouTube, 1 min., 47 sec., https://www.youtube.com/watch?v=2J4yJXYPJDw.
13. Isaac Boaheng and Justice Korankye, "A Christian View of Stewardship: A Study of Daniel 6:1–4," *E-Journal of Religious and Theological Studies* 8, no. 6 (2022): 156–65, https://noyam.org/wp-content/uploads/2022/07/ERATS2022862.pdf.
14. Personal communication with the author.

Chapter 13: Another Look

1. "*Agamemnon*: Lines 914–1071," Sparknotes, accessed May 2, 2025, https://www.sparknotes.com/lit/agamemnon/section5/.
2. Renan Botelho, "The History and Evolution of the Red Carpet: From Ancient Greece to Modern Hollywood," *Women's Wear Daily*, October 5, 2023, https://wwd.com/feature/red-carpet-history-1235839803/.
3. Elijah Chiland, "6 Things You Didn't Know About the Oscars Red

Carpet," Curbed LA, February 26, 2017, https://la.curbed.com/2017/2/26/14745794/oscars-academy-awards-red-carpet.
4. Irmo Marini, "The History of Treatment Toward People with Disabilities," in *Psychosocial Aspects of Disability*, 2nd ed., ed. Irmo Marini et al. (Springer, 2017), https://connect.springerpub.com/content/book/978-0-8261-8063-6/part/part01/chapter/ch01.
5. Smitty, "The Red Carpet at the Oscars Costs How Much?," 101.5 WPDH, February 14, 2019, https://wpdh.com/the-red-carpet-at-the-oscars-costs-how-much/.
6. *New Testament Greek Lexicon—KJV*, "Trecho," Bible Study Tools, accessed May 2, 2025, https://www.biblestudytools.com/lexicons/greek/kjv/trecho.html.

ABOUT THE AUTHORS

TIM TEBOW IS A SPEAKER, ENTREPRENEUR, COLLEGE football analyst for ESPN and the SEC Network, and author of five *New York Times* bestsellers, including *Shaken*, *This Is the Day*, and the children's book series *Bronco and Friends*. Prior to his current endeavors, Tim was an NFL quarterback, a two-time NCAAF national champion, a Heisman Trophy winner, and a College Football Hall of Fame inductee.

He's also the founder of the Tim Tebow Foundation, dedicated to bringing Faith, Hopew and Love to those needing a brighter day in their darkest hour of need. Since 2010, the foundation has served some of the world's Most Vulnerable People—the real MVPs—across more than one hundred countries through ministry focuses in Anti-Human Trafficking and Child Exploitation, Orphan Care and Prevention, Profound Medical Needs, and Special Needs.

Tim is married to Demi-Leigh Tebow, who is a speaker, author, entrepreneur, and Miss Universe 2017. They live in Jacksonville, Florida, with their daughter, Daphne Reign, and their three dogs, Chunk, Kobe, and Paris.

A.J. GREGORY IS A SEASONED COLLABORATIVE VOICE who has written, edited, or contributed to more than sixty books, several of which have earned *New York Times* bestseller status. She partners with a wide range of voices, including professional athletes, military leaders, scientists, natural health experts, and entrepreneurs. A.J. lives in New Jersey with her husband, Jabazz, and their three children.

The next stop was on the second floor of a dilapidated apartment building. Like the previous home, this one was a testament to survival amid chaos. The room was so small that some of our team had to stay in the hallway. More conversation. More prayer. More glimpses into the profound needs of those created as God's image. My heart grew heavier. Seeing people living in squalor hits hard. It drove home the reality that poverty wasn't an occasional hardship for them; it was their everyday life.

As we said our goodbyes, I led the team down the stairs toward the front doors of the apartment. The moment my foot hit the tile at the bottom step, I noticed a large crowd gathered outside. Filipinos, in my experience, love Americans, and their curiosity had likely drawn them here after hearing about our visit.

Before I could take another step, a burly man surged through the crowd, a little kid in his arms. He shoved the boy toward me, pleading in broken English. The noise of the crowd made it hard to understand him. "Please," he said, gesturing frantically. Then I caught a word. "Hospital," the man said, pointing to the little boy. When I looked at the child, I noticed something wrong with his arm. It was bent unnaturally, twisted behind his back as if it had been broken and never healed. When I looked down, I noticed more. One of the boy's feet was clubbed. The man, clutching his hands together, continued to plead. I caught more words: "Hospital. Tebow. Cure."

The pieces began to fit. The man must have heard of the Tebow Cure Hospital and recognized me as someone who could help. I later learned this child with disabilities was his nephew. When I finally realized what the man was asking, I was overwhelmed. *Could I help care for his nephew? Could I do something to alleviate the boy's suffering? Could I be the hope he was desperately seeking?* With the help of translators, we got the uncle's information and connected him with the hospital.